A Sense of Sociology

A SENSE OF SOCIOLOGY

Lee Braude

PRAEGER PUBLISHERS

New York · Washington

To the Memory of My Father

Published in the United States of America in 1974
by Praeger Publishers, Inc.
111 Fourth Avenue, New York, N.Y. 10003

© 1974 by Praeger Publishers, Inc.

Library of Congress Cataloging in Publication Data

Braude, Lee.
    A sense of sociology.

    (Viewpoints in sociology)
    Bibliography: p. 145.
    1. Sociology.   I.   Title.
HM51.B8   301   72-80451

Printed in the United States of America

Contents

Editor's Foreword

by Jerry D. Rose

VIEWPOINTS IN SOCIOLOGY is intended to make available to the beginning student of sociology a series of provocative treatises in the several areas of sociological study. One purpose of the series is to demonstrate the fallacy of the aphorism "Short writing makes long reading." Authors were given the difficult task of covering the major areas of their topic succinctly, but without producing an overly terse treatment. This could be accomplished only through the exercise of a keen sense of the sociologically relevant—an ability to separate the quick from the dead and the essential from the trivial. The model is analogous to that of the successful classroom lecturer who is faced with the need to present a seemingly infinite amount of material in a decidedly finite amount of time. It is, then, not coincidental that the authors in this series are gifted teachers as well as scholars.

Within the broad mandate outlined above, each author was encouraged to give his or her essay whatever individual slant was considered appropriate to the subject. Completely detached analysis is not one of the goals of the series. If the writers sometimes display passion and commitment, this is because sociology is itself a variety of human behavior.

The keynote volume of the series, Lee Braude's A SENSE OF SOCIOLOGY, is the work of a dedicated scholar-teacher determined to demonstrate by his own involvement in the field the "sense" that is made of sociology by those who are professionally committed to it. His aim is not to make professional sociologists of his readers. Rather, it is to produce a greater "appreciation" of professional sociology, not for the purpose of enhancing the sociologist's ego, but in order to enhance the student's awareness of worlds of social experience beyond that of his chosen occupation, community, and family. The professor of sociology who believes that his discipline can contribute to this wider human consciousness will ask his students to read this work.

Preface and Acknowledgments

THIS IS NOT a sociology textbook. There are quite enough of those. The intent of this book is more modest: it presents one sociologist's view of the problems, prospects, and pleasures of sociology. The book is based on the premise that the field of sociology is more than a collection of facts or theories or even opinions. An understanding of sociology provides, in my view, an unparalleled avenue to an appreciation of man both as independent agent and in cooperative activity with others. The more we can learn about human conduct, the more we ultimately learn about ourselves. And in a world that appears to be but a procession of crises, this knowledge, that humans are unique and yet alike, may be all that holds us together. For this reason, a sociological sense is not only revealing, not only exciting; at this time it is critical.

I hope to appeal to the college student who, though nurtured in skepticism, is alive to ideas and change. Whether he takes one sociology course or many, he will find in the sociological orientation a reasoned and reasonable approach to change that may aid him in confronting his world—as it is and as he might wish it to be. I hope the reader will sense my conviction that we cannot turn away from the only life we have. We must live that life, embracing it fully and passionately. But we must also know something about the ways in which man adapts to his world before we can choose a particular style or variety of life to make our own. Out of the disciplined inquiry of sociology comes an awareness of the many designs for living available to us. Such awareness can offer hope. If for no other reason, the practice of sociology is a worthwhile endeavor.

I want now to recognize those who, in one way or another, have contributed their insights and talents to the development of this volume, fully acknowledging at the same time that its faults and shortcomings are all mine. The late Louis Wirth and Philip M. Hauser (who is very much alive) are my models of the sociological stance; their uncommon blend of scholarship with action has influenced my own development far more than I can possibly describe, and I am so very pleased to be able to record my debt to them here. From Oscar Shabat, Meyer Weinberg, and the distinguished sociologist Everett C. Hughes I learned just how exciting, rewarding, and demanding the role of the teacher-scholar can be. I thank my dear friend and colleague Jerry D. Rose for his encouragement and stimulation. Arthur J. Vidich brought his own grace and style to bear, though unobtrusively, on much of the undertaking. Thanks are due as well to my colleague Edward Ludwig and to the Executive Office of the American Sociological Association for information provided. Special thanks are due to Gladys Topkis, my editor at Praeger, who took this volume under her wing and from start to finish guided the project with warmth and exuberance—even when the blue pencil ran freely. Finally, but most important, I thank my wife, Norma, and my son, Jeffrey, for being who they are and where they are. Their presence makes my efforts all the more worthwhile.

Fredonia, New York   LEE BRAUDE
August, 1973

A Sense of Sociology

1

The Science of Sociology

One generation passeth away, and another generation cometh; time and chance happeneth to them all.

—Ecclesiastes

Since 'tis Nature's law to change,
Constancy alone is strange.
—Earl of Rochester, John Wilmot

For as long as there have been humans on this planet there has been change. And for that long humans have tried to understand the changes they saw. Love and birth and death. Harvest and floodtide. Eclipse and earthquake. The changes people saw about them might have been too difficult or too awful or too bewildering to comprehend, but, as far as we know, every age has wrestled with the problem of change in order that life might have some meaning, some sense of direction and purpose—however unclear that direction might be.

In addition to the problem of change, the historical record suggests that human beings have for centuries been confronted by the persistent tension between the one and the many, between the individual's search for his own autonomy and his involvement in an environment that might deprive him of his autonomy and his sense of uniqueness. The age-old question "Am I my brother's keeper?" seems forever to recur. And to this question, too, the human species has had to find—and must find today—some answer.

In these pages I hope to share my excitement about one way of understanding the world and man's place within it. Certainly, sociology is not the only way. It may not even be the "best" way. But I am convinced that the approach sociology offers makes it possible to confront the complexity of life in a less confusing fashion and to see some hope where there might otherwise be discouragement.

In this first chapter I try to set forth the guiding assumptions and point of view of the field of sociology. In Chapter 2 I attempt to show how sociology emerged out of centuries of speculation about the social character of men, to demonstrate that the sociological perspective is part of man's continuing quest to understand himself and the human condition. Chapter 3 explores the questions: who are sociologists and what do they do? How do they put sociology into practice? Chapter 4 examines three results of sociological inquiry—a study of suicide, an examination of life in a slum, and a research report on the relation between religious identification and worldly success. In Chapter 5, finally, I consider the question: what does it all mean?

Sociology is one current outcome of man's unceasing attempt to understand himself. It begins with the premise that the one inescapable fact of human existence is that man is born into and lives out his life in groups. It is obvious that it takes two to conceive him, and it takes considerably more than his parents to turn a little bundle of protoplasm into a thinking, responding, functioning adult. The sociologist takes the position that it is the relations one forms with others—however enduring or transitory these relations may be—that provide the context for this remarkable metamorphosis and that, in fact, give every person his distinctive characteristics, that make him different from all those who have ever lived, are living now, or ever will live in the future. This necessary involvement of the human being in groups the sociologist takes as his starting point.

But look at what man starts with. When you think about it, being human is a remarkable capacity. The species that has produced a Beethoven and a Newton has also produced a Herod and a Hitler. What other creature—as far as we know —can hope and dream and anticipate? Who else but this earth-linked being can grope toward the stars and, perhaps, actually reach them, as he has reached the moon?

The human animal differs from his nonhuman relatives not only in degree but in kind; he is not necessarily a larger animal, nor is he different solely by virtue of his greater biological complexity; he is a different being altogether. Certainly, *homo sapiens* can stand upright. Among all animals only he has an opposable thumb—a finger that can be moved opposite to all other fingers so as to afford greater grasping and manipulative ability. And man has the most complex nervous system so far discovered. However, it is what the human does with all these attributes that is amazing. One could say that the behavioral potentialities of nonhuman members of the animal kingdom are literally programed into their neuromuscular order. The courting mechanism of peacocks, the spawning habits of Columbia River salmon, and the nest-building of robins occur in precisely the same way from individual to individual and from generation to generation. No member of the species need "learn" the behavior. It is simply "there"; it is instinctive. But consider a human building his "nest" in the Sahara or in Kobe, Japan, or in Larkspur, California. Or consider differences in eating or even the varieties of behavior preliminary to sexual intercourse in different parts of the world or different segments of

the same society. Such a multiplicity of behavioral forms suggests the astonishing plasticity of the human organism—and
its amazing potential, limited only by genetic and constitu-
tional capacity (and, of course, by social and cultural constraints, although those are not our concern at this point).

Even this does not tell the full story. The human does not
simply respond or react to the world about him. He *creates*
his world. He need not hibernate for a season to escape the
cold; nor need he suffer extreme heat or even darkness: he
shuts out the elements by wearing clothes and building
houses. He can transmit the results of his experience—his fail-
ures as well as his successes—to men yet to be born. To the
history of the animal species embedded in their genetic structures, the human animal adds the cumulative record of experience, added layer upon layer since the first man set an uncer-
tain foot upon the forest floor. Whether the record be written
or passed by word of mouth, every people lives with mem-
ories that provide a reason for being and, perhaps, a rationale
for change. Man has been called a "time-binding creature"[1]
because he compresses in his present his recognition of his
past, however sketchy it may be, and his hopes, plans, and
perceptions of his future. Thus, you attend college not only
because you wish to fulfill your parents' dreams (your past)
but also because you have some dreams of your own (your
future). Your choice of major may be one that will not only
satisfy your intellectual curiosity now but also permit you to
find a job that will satisfy you (and, perhaps, your parents)
in the future. Thus, you plan accordingly. And this, so far as
we know, no other animal can do.

Obviously, then, "being human" must be something more
than a matter of posture or thumb or brain. In the final

[1] Alfred Korzybski, *Manhood of Humanity* (New York: E. P. Dut-
ton, 1921), pp. 3 ff., 67; *idem, Time-Binding* (New York: E. P. Dut-
ton, 1924); and *idem, Science and Sanity* (New York: International
Non-Aristotelian Library, 1948). The base of this "time-binding" com-
pression is, of course, language.

analysis, it boils down to the fact that man and only man has "culture." A famous anthropologist, Alfred L. Kroeber, coined the word "superorganic" to apply to this distinctively human attribute, which overlays the organic quality of *homo sapiens* much as clothing covers flesh.[2] Some have called it a "design for living,"[3] others the "art, artifacts, and idea systems of a people,"[4] and still others refer to culture as the "total way of life of a people."[5] However culture is defined, it is ultimately symbolic in character, for it depends on language. Without a set of ideas, there can be no culture. Consequently, the group life of man is ultimately a symbolic life, and man may be said to exist in and through his ability to communicate symbolically,[6] i.e., through language.

[2] A. L. Kroeber, "The Superorganic," *American Anthropologist* (New Series) 19 (April–June, 1917): 163–213.

[3] Clyde Kluckhohn, "The Study of Culture," in Lewis A. Coser and Bernard Rosenberg, eds., *Sociological Theory: A Book of Readings* (New York: Macmillan, 1957), pp. 49–63.

[4] Edward B. Tylor, "Culture Defined," in *ibid.*, pp. 18–21.

[5] Clyde Kluckhohn, *Mirror for Man* (New York: McGraw-Hill, 1948), p. 17.

[6] The discussion that follows is based largely on the writings of George Herbert Mead. Mead (1863–1931) was a philosopher in the tradition of William James and John Dewey, with whom he taught at the University of Chicago. This tradition, pragmatism, asserts that knowledge, belief, values do not exist, as it were, "out there" in the world, apart from people. Rather, they take shape only through the experiences of individuals acting on a world that, in turn, acts back on them. Ultimately, the person and his world are socially constituted or constructed; each represents a different level of analysis of ongoing interpersonal experience (see Darnell Rucker, *The Chicago Pragmatists* [Minneapolis: University of Minnesota Press, 1969], pp. 28–56; and Charles Morris, *The Pragmatic Movement in American Philosophy* [New York: George Braziller, 1970]). Moreover, the morality or efficacy of values or action cannot be seen apart from the goals toward which the actor moves.

Like the other exponents of the pragmatist view, Mead came to pragmatism through an attempt to deal with the ageless "mind-body" problem. The question had usually been posed in terms of hierarchy: did the mind control the body, or vice versa? The pragmatists argued that such an orientation was fallacious. Rather, "mind" and "body" should be viewed as two aspects of a process in which, again, the acting individual is central; through action each is transformed by the other. That is, as environment (including other humans) creates the organism (or person), so does the organism create the environment. For Mead it was a short intellectual jump to the assertion that *individual* psychological activity is really *social* psychological activity; and it has been asserted that his course in social psychology represented the flowering of his perspective (Morris, *Pragmatic Movement*, p. 188). To put it very simply, Mead maintained that the individual comes into society, and society into the individual, when the person acquires a repertoire of symbols. As he manipulates these symbols, as he uses language, he learns the intentions of others, including the generalized expectations of society. He incorporates the demands of others into his own behavior and consequently learns to exercise upon himself as an adult the controls exercised by others when he was a child. He becomes aware of himself when he realizes that he can be both the subject and object of his behavior, when he can respond to himself as others respond to him, and thus can see himself from the standpoint of others involved in relations with him. Human behavior, in this view, is not simply a response to stimulus but a continual working out of one's encounter with his environment, both of people and of things—interpreting and defining the implications of this encounter for the forward motion of the person. This orientation in sociology has come to be known as *symbolic interactionism*.

In an age when "publish or perish" is the guide to survival of the academic, it is difficult to believe that Mead wrote little; he was much happier lecturing in the classroom. His major works—*Mind, Self and Society; Philosophy of the Act;* and *Movements of Thought in the Nineteenth Century*—are largely stenographic notes commissioned by devoted students. All three were published posthumously. Mead influenced sociology essentially through the students who came to his classes and who used his ideas in their own work. See, for example, Herbert Blumer, "Social Psychology," in Emerson P. Schmidt, ed., *Man and Society: A Substantive Introduction to the Social Sciences* (New York: Prentice-Hall, 1938), pp. 144–98; Herbert Blumer, *Symbolic Interactionism: Perspective and Method* (Englewood Cliffs, N.J.: Prentice-Hall, 1969); Lewis A. Coser, *Masters of Sociological Thought* (New York: Harcourt Brace Jovanovich, 1971), pp. 333–55; Jerome G. Manis and Bernard N. Meltzer, eds., *Symbolic Interaction: A Reader in Theory and Method*, 2d ed. (Boston: Allyn & Bacon, 1972); Paul E. Pfuetze, *Self, Society, Existence* (New York: Harper, 1961); Arnold Rose, "A Systematic Summary of Symbolic Interaction Theory," in Arnold M. Rose, ed., *Human Behavior and Social Processes: An Interactionist Approach* (Boston: Houghton Mifflin, 1962), pp. 3–19; and Anselm L. Strauss, *Mirrors and Masks: The Search for Identity* (Glencoe, Ill.: Free Press, 1959).

This may appear to be a rather strong statement. But consider what a symbol is. A symbol represents or stands for something else. It is not a reproduction of the thing, but a representation. The letters *c, h, a, i, r* don't look anything like your mother's prize Chippendale in the dining room or that chrome-and-leather Eames version in your own living room. But we "know" that those five letters—*c, h, a, i, r*—refer to something we sit on and not to something we eat on or (except in unusual circumstances) something to be thrown into a fireplace. Moreover, the symbol is an arbitrary designation; there is no inherent relation between the symbol and the object it represents. The object we sit on is called a *Stuhl* in German and a *kisay* in Hebrew; for that matter, it could be a "riahc" if we so chose. Even in a situation where the word for a sound—"hiss," let us say—may sound like the sound, the object to which the symbol refers (a sound symbolic of antagonism toward something or someone) need not be immediately present for us to act with reference to it. We are able to develop high orders of abstractions—like the "square root of −1," "ghosts," or "love"—without being able to point out a concrete referent. (When was the last time you saw a ghost?)

In addition—and a very important addition at that—symbols have plans of action built into them. They tell us what to do to or with the object of reference. The "meaning" of a symbol is that our "plan of action" is like others' so that joint action becomes possible. This is what the philosophers mean when they talk about a "universe of discourse." The word "baby," for example, suggests a new member of the species who is to be fondled, maintained, and protected rather than eaten or hurled against the wall. (When such horrors happen, the question is often raised: "What did that baby mean to the person who did that?") We assume that others will see the baby in the same light as we, and so we entrust the child to a babysitter for an evening or to its grandparents for a week.

Moreover, because we have learned what response to make, and because our responses will predictably (in most cases) be like others', objects need not be present for us to act toward them as if they were. Thus, when that baby of ours is at his grandparents', his parents can speculate on his actions at that very moment or even "see" the little bundle of joy, no matter how far away he is. Because human behavior is symbolic behavior, our actions need not be automatic. We may delay them or, as George Herbert Mead put it, hold these actions in suspension,[7] that is, complete the action internally "in our heads"—try it out—before acting overtly. We may internally assess or question the significance of the behavior of others or our own behavior. By approaching others symbolically, we approach ourselves in the same way, because we use assumptions about their behavior toward us as cues for our own behavior. We can stand back and look at ourselves, question our motives, and evaluate alternative modes of conduct before (or, for that matter, after) we commit ourselves to public behavior. How often do we say to ourselves: "I should never have done that," or "I want to do this, but I know what the consequences are," or "I don't want to hurt her, but she'd better hear it from me. I'll tell her—tomorrow." "I bombed." "I was the hit of the party!" Following Mead, some have argued that it is this ability to act back on oneself, this reflexive or self-stimulating quality, that is the hallmark of the human state.

The fact that human life is symbolic life is at once the curse and the promise of human association. If you think about it, the tensions that exist between individuals and groups are more often than not symbolically rooted. Different symbol sets provide different ways of looking at the world. And the world as seen by each of the parties to a

---

[7] George H. Mead, *Mind, Self and Society* (Chicago: University of Chicago Press, 1934), pp. 90–100; *idem, The Philosophy of the Act* (Chicago: University of Chicago Press, 1938), pp. 4–8, 131–53.

transaction becomes a different world. The slurs leveled by one group at another, the "generation gap" between the teenager or young adult and his parents or teachers, the dilemma of international cooperation in the age of overkill, all bespeak the immense problem that obtains when "my world" is pitted against "your world." Now, no one would suggest that a crash course in "communications skills" will result in "our world"; the modification of opposing views is not that simple. But some approach to consensus in the use of symbols is an absolute prerequisite to common action. And the longer such agreement can be maintained, the easier it is to share, to develop a sense of common enterprise, perhaps to love.[8]

If, then, you are willing to grant the importance of symbols for the life of man, it becomes necessary to ask how symbols become part of man's environment. The answer to this question will bring us directly to the domain of the sociologist.

It is obvious that symbols do not exist "out there" in the environment waiting to be absorbed by a pliant mind, as snowflakes whirling about are later absorbed by the wool on which they fall. It is equally obvious that the human individual is not born with a repertoire of symbols. He must learn them. They become part of his experience by virtue of the association of the individual with others. I said before that the one inescapable fact of human existence is our necessary involvement in groups. Denied this association, for all his resemblance to others around him, a member of our species would simply not be human, for his symbolic repertoire would be meager and possibly nonexistent. (Descriptions of feral children, children who—like the "wild boy of Aveyron" or "Isabel"—were unwanted and abandoned and consequently spent their early years in isolation, deprived of human relationships, bear out this contention.)[9]

[8] See Kurt Riezler, *Man: Mutable and Immutable* (Chicago: Henry Regnery, 1950).
[9] Kingsley Davis, "Final Note on a Case of Extreme Isolation,"

The human being is born helpless, and he remains so for a longer period than any other animal. He will not survive unless aided. This requires the presence of others. And the individual, says the sociologist, will need others throughout his life. Consequently, sociology may be viewed as that intellectual discipline (and we use both words advisedly) which asks—and attempts to answer—two separate but crucially interrelated questions. First, what are the implications of man's group membership for his individual life? The second question, which follows logically from the first, is this: Given the fact that men are the products of group life, how is it possible for them to cooperate in order to achieve common ends? How wonderful it is for people from different backgrounds, with different heritages and experiences, to be able to come together and jointly achieve some common purpose —a class in a college, the construction of a house, the growth of affection between a man and a woman. It is wonderful and remarkable, but at the same time it is an everyday occurrence, which makes it possible to carry on the work of the world. The sociologist wants to know how this, too, happens. In short, sociology is concerned with the ways in which the person achieves both his particular distinctiveness and the similarity to others that makes cooperative living possible. The sociologist would argue that it is the group that provides the context for differences as well as likeness, because it is in the group that one encounters symbols. Even if one is alone, the use of language—making indications to oneself—is tantamount to making indications to another; thus, others may be presumed to be involved even in solitude—or loneliness.

American Journal of Sociology 50 (March, 1947): 432–37. See also *idem*, "Extreme Social Isolation of a Child," *American Journal of Sociology* 45 (January, 1940): 554–64; William F. Ogburn, "The Wolf Boy of Agra," *American Journal of Sociology* 54 (March, 1959): 449–54; and J. A. L. Singh and Robert M. Zingg, *Wolf-Children and Feral Man* (New York: Harper, 1939).

But why should the group be the vehicle for the human drama? In a way, the group is a byproduct or an outcome of the uncertainty or problematic character of existence. The helplessness of the infant persists to some degree throughout life, for no human is completely self-sufficient. When we encounter a situation in which our own abilities or insights are wanting, so that resolution of the situation requires the aid of others, then a group is formed when we enter into distinctive social relations with these others, whether the number be one or twenty. To be sure, the "problem" may be nothing more than asking directions in a strange town, or it may be as momentous as international meetings on which the fate of the world depends. As long as one needs help, a relation ensues and a group is formed.[10] Now, a social relation depends upon the mutual recognition and response of each to the other. This recognition need not be accurate. It is necessary only that the participants behave *as if* it were (and in this is the nub of prejudice, of the stereotype, of interpersonal tensions). Consequently, social life—or, more specifically, group life—is symbolic life.

There is, however, another, more practical reason why sociology lays claim to group (or social) relations as its area of concern. All the fields that are traditionally subsumed under the heading of "social sciences"—economics, political science, anthropology, psychology, and the like—purport to study human (or primate, in the case of anthropology) social behavior. The sociologist counters this contention by pointing out that these fields tend to split apart such behavior. There is no behavior that is political and that only, or economic and that only, or even cultural and that only. The sociologist sug-

[10] This statement is based in part on Robert M. MacIver and Charles H. Page, *Society: An Introductory Analysis*, rev. ed. (New York: Rinehart, 1949), p. 14, and on the work of Robert F. Bales, who has investigated the dynamics of small groups. See Robert F. Bales, "A Set of Categories for the Analysis of Small Group Interaction," *American Sociological Review* 15 (April, 1950): 257–63.

gests (and at an earlier stage in the history of sociology the suggestion was so vehemently offered that it bordered on a challenge to a back-alley brawl) that human conduct must be understood as a totality. He argues that this totality is no more and no less than the group behavior itself, which provides a framework for the content—political, cultural, etc. —of that behavior.[11]

So it is, then, that the sociologist turns to the forms of human association or, as he calls it, human interaction. How do people relate to one another, how do they interact, and what general statements can we make about the ways in which they do so? The notion of a general statement is crucial here, because if sociology is in fact a science rather than a collection of platitudes or moral exhortations, it is able to generalize by relating classes of phenomena that exhibit similar characteristics and to predict on the basis of these similarities. For example, if I know something about a college class in the French language and something about a college class in introductory biology and something about a college class in general chemistry, I ought to be able to say something about college classes in general and consequently to predict what I may find in a college class in sociology or calculus or music education. If you think about it, science is simply the technique by which the investigator hopes to generate knowledge that relates what he has discovered to what is already known and what could conceivably be known in the future, and to do so in as precise and rigorous a fashion as possible. Science is simply one way of knowing,

[11] The nature of the debate is suggested by Dennis H. Wrong, "The Oversocialized Conception of Man in Modern Sociology," *American Sociological Review* 26 (April, 1961): 183–93; Charles K. Warriner, "Groups Are Real: A Reaffirmation," *American Sociological Review* 21 (October, 1956): 549–54; Robert E. Park and Ernest W. Burgess, *Introduction to the Science of Sociology* (Chicago: University of Chicago Press, 1921), pp. 1–57; and Roscoe C. Hinkle, Jr., and Gisela J. Hinkle, *The Development of Modern Sociology* (New York: Random House, 1954), pp. 1–28.

and any particular science, like sociology, becomes a special case of that way.[12]

Sociologists subscribe to the assumptions of science. They are committed to the discovery of knowledge and synthesis of knowledge, not only because they are gratified and fascinated by the search itself and believe that the knowledge is worth getting, but also because they believe that in getting it they are adding to the total fund of human understanding about the world, which might make that world a little less dark and forbidding. Scientists are incurable optimists. They operate on the assumption that knowledge does in fact make a difference. Perhaps what they learn will be used by others; perhaps this knowledge may gather dust on a library shelf. But the fact that by their efforts the obscure becomes less so is reason enough to continue to hammer away at the unknown.

In searching for general, predictable statements about social behavior, the sociologist would appear to be in a far more precarious position than the natural or physical scientist, because human behavior seems to be so irrational and, hence, unpredictable. Yet consider the fact that, while it may be difficult to predict the activity of a particular molecule of a gas, the behavior of the gas in general can be predicted on the basis of what is known about its constituents. Or the fact that, while we may not be able to indicate the marginal error of a device that measures, say, electrical energy, we can certainly read the dial on the device and make some predictions about the lethal potential of that energy. In other words, there is a degree of "unpredictability" about all phenomena, be they physical or social; the knowledge that we have of such phenomena is not only provisional and tentative—state-

[12] With respect to sociology, see Morton M. Hunt, "Profiles: How Does It Come to Be So?" *New Yorker* 36 (January 28, 1961): 32–44, 49–63, a brief biography of Robert K. Merton, an eminent sociologist noted especially for his efforts to bring sociological research into greater harmony with developing sociological theory.

ments accepted today may be the errors of tomorrow—but also only "probable." "Truth" is a matter of faith. We live in a probabilistic universe, where there are no "yesses" or "noes" but only "maybes." The scientist, recognizing this, attempts to make certain that his approach to his data is responsive enough to yield results that will maximize his predictive capabilities, that will give him the highest probability that a will in fact give rise to b.

Without feeling the least bit defensive, then, the sociologist acknowledges the probabilistic character of his data about human interaction. He recognizes that his task at this juncture is to collect the most reliable body of information about interaction that it is possible to obtain. He tries for general statements only with respect to the body of data at hand, or statements that may relate bodies of similar data. Prediction at higher levels of generality must, he knows, wait for more knowledge. And most sociologists are, in fact, currently engaged in the very exciting and appealing business of finding out about the social world.

But it is a dirty business as well. Gathering knowledge about one's fellows can be threatening or intimidating to those studied and productive of considerable suspicion about the motives of the researcher. The sociologist has often been described as a kind of "intellectual peeping Tom" who is at his best when searching out the seamier sides of people's activities. In the earlier chapters of the history of the field, sociologists were accused of being "do-gooders" at best and, at the worst, Marxist sympathizers.[13] They may be either of

[13] See Hinkle and Hinkle, *Development of Modern Sociology*, pp. 12–14; Joseph Wood Krutch, "Through Happiness with Slide Rule and Calipers," *Saturday Review* 46 (November 2, 1961): 12–15; Russell Kirk, "Is Social Science Scientific?" *New York Times Magazine*, June 25, 1961, pp. 11, 15–16, 18; Robert K. Merton, "Now the Case *for* Sociology," *New York Times Magazine*, July 16, 1961, pp. 14, 19–21; Russell Kirk *et al.*, "Battle of Sociology (Continued)," *New York Times Magazine*, July 23, 1961, pp. 30–31; and Alfred deGrazia, "The Hatred of New Social Science," *American Behavioral Scientist* 5 (October, 1961): 5–13.

these, or neither; like the members of any other calling, they vary in political persuasion, interest in the underdog, and many other characteristics. The sociologist is simply intensely curious, however much the roots of his curiosity may be suspect.

To satisfy this curiosity, sociologists find their data anywhere human beings come together: in an operating theater, in the relation between janitor and tenant, among ditchdiggers, in an employees' cafeteria, between a prostitute and her pimp. What turns an observation of behavior into a socially relevant observation is the particular point of view of the sociologist—his perspective or his imagination, if you will.[14]

This perspective is neither marvelous nor strange. It differs from common sense only in that the sociologist comes with a set of questions to ask of his observations and a set of categories to organize what he sees. When guided by the rules and logic of science, the sociologist can be reasonably certain that his findings will add to the body of sociological knowledge, that they will be something more than either idle speculation or educated guesses.

Let us look first at method.[15] Any scholarly research begins with a kind of intellectual itch—something that bothers us and about which we might want to know more. We may not

[14] See C. Wright Mills, *The Sociological Imagination* (London and New York: Oxford University Press, 1959). This volume has become a virtual classic. See also, on the operating room, Erving Goffman, *Encounters: Two Studies in the Sociology of Interaction* (Indianapolis: Bobbs-Merrill, 1961), pp. 115–32; on janitors and tenants, Ray Gold, "Janitors *vs.* Tenants: A Status-Income Dilemma," *American Journal of Sociology* 57 (March, 1952): 486–93; on ditchdiggers, Richard R. Myers, "Interpersonal Relations in the Building Industry," *Applied Anthropology* 5 (Spring, 1946): 1–7; on prostitutes, James H. Bryan, "Apprenticeships in Prostitution," *Social Problems* 12 (Winter, 1965): 287–97.

[15] See, for example, Stephen Cole, *The Sociological Method* (Chicago: Markham, 1972); John Madge, *The Origins of Scientific Sociology* (Glencoe, Ill.: Free Press, 1962); and Robert Bierstedt, ed., *A Design for Sociology: Scope, Objectives, and Methods* (Philadelphia: American Academy of Political and Social Science, 1969).

even be able to state it in formal terms—that comes later—but we at least recognize the existence of a problem that might be worth looking at in an attempt to solve it. Then we start reading to see what others have said about our interest. Now, it very well may be that, in the course of our reading, we come upon some writer who answers our questions satisfactorily and thereby solves the problem. But, for the sake of discussion, let us assume the far more interesting situation in which we read and read but the answer nonetheless eludes us. We must now ask ourselves how we would approach the problem. First we must be able to state the problem clearly and unambiguously. Statement of the problem in itself may tell us how it could be solved. When we have once been able to do that, then we are in a position to begin to focus on the solution.

The first step involves an attempt to place the by now well-specified problem in the larger perspective of what is known about the problem and to manipulate the perspective in such a way that new light is shed on that problem. The scholar is provoked into thinking about it in new and perhaps unanticipated ways, and possible roads to solution open up. This step constitutes the development of what is sometimes called a *theoretical orientation,* a detailed description of the kind of intellectual apparatus with which the investigator will work. (This, incidentally, is one definition of "theory.")[16] Within this orientation the researcher presents his conception of the meaningful variables—or those factors that should be considered in his problem—and possible relations between them, relations that could be tested to see if they do really exist and, consequently, provide the answers to the problem.

The use of the term "variables" and the reference to the investigator's attempt to specify possible relations between

[16] Presented by Louis Wirth in his classes. For a brief and entertaining discussion of scientific method, see Garvin McCain and Erwin M. Segal, *The Game of Science* (Belmont, Calif.: Brooks/Cole, 1969).

variables at the very outset of his inquiry should suggest that the thinking of the sociologist is mathematically oriented. Science demands precision, and mathematics constitutes the tool by which this precision can be both achieved and maintained. Further, since the sociologist recognizes that he operates within a world of probabilities where nothing is wholly "yes" or "no" but only possible or potential, he wants to use those techniques that enable him to make the broadest and yet most precise statements of relationship of which he is capable, given the current state of the art. He therefore uses what can be extremely sophisticated statistical techniques of inference and proof, which, of course, depend on and use mathematical operations. Whether or not the scientist deals with quantitative phenomena, his imagery is always mathematical. That is, he views the changeability of social phenomena as being susceptible to numerical expression and believes that the intensity, direction, and persistence of these relationships can be quantitatively ordered, tested, and predicted. Wherever possible, then, sociology is experimental in outlook; the individual sociologist wants to test his notions to see whether they hold up and to explain his findings as simply and as judiciously as possible. However, at the same time he wants to tie his statements to what is already known on the subject.

If the investigator suggests in his theoretical orientation some new solution to his problem, he is obviously interested in finding out whether his assumptions can withstand detailed scrutiny. He therefore proposes a *hypothesis*, a relationship between variables stated in a form suitable for testing, and proceeds to develop a *research design* to test that hypothesis. And when he has done so, he presents his *conclusions*, which indicate not only what he has found but where he went wrong and, perhaps most important, how the job might be done better by a subsequent researcher. He does all this not merely to ventilate his spleen or to publicly voice a *mea culpa* but because the most severe test of any scientist-sociologist's work is the evaluation of his colleagues, his peers. Unless a scientist is willing to have his work evaluated, perhaps even redone, by others and unless he openly details the process by which he worked, he is a charlatan. If science is a method by which one rigorously searches for the best available evidence, the scientist must be willing to offer his work to public scrutiny so that his scholarly community may weigh the elegance of his findings and the quality of the data-gathering process. The scientist, the sociologist, is always on trial before the harshest jury of all, his professional peers.

As we have seen, then, sociologists operate with the imagery of mathematics as they plan and carry out their research. But this imagery is not unique to sociology among the social sciences. What differentiates sociological inquiry from the enterprises of other social sciences is the focus of the scientific method upon human interaction itself. What is the impact of the forms of association assumed by humans upon the individual and upon an organized social life, without which the work of the world could not be accomplished? This concern with interaction—as it were, without content (other social sciences study that content)—gives sociology its breadth of interest and provides the rationale for the particular questions the sociologist brings to his research. The questions, in turn, structure sociological application of the scientific method.[17] At every point in his investigation, the sociologist asks three questions about what he is doing. First, what are the *units of interaction?* What kinds of entities are participating in the interaction? Are they individuals, cliques, classes, gangs, families, nations? If I can say something about these entities, am I in a better position to say something constructive and generalizable about the interaction that ensues? Second, the sociologist asks about the *process of*

[17] See Kurt H. Wolff, ed. and trans., *The Sociology of Georg Simmel* (Glencoe, Ill.: Free Press, 1950), esp. pp. 21 ff.

interaction. What are the components or phases of the process? Can we chart it? Does it resemble other processes about which we already know? For example, are the ways in which college students go about choosing friends at all similar to the ways in which coal miners or salesmen or the elderly choose friends? Is there a common thread running through all these interactions which we can call "friendship"? Are the components of "friendship" at all related to the components of "love," on the one hand, and of toadying, on the other? Finally, sociologists are concerned with what can be called the *matrix of interaction*—that is, the physical or social space in which the interaction occurs. Consider the setting and behavioral expectations of a party, a funeral, a poker game. The more information we have about these settings, the better able we should be to understand the interaction that takes place in such "locations."[18]

In addition, the sociologist continuously questions the adequacy of the research endeavor itself. He is concerned about the *validity* of his research. Is he measuring or testing what he expects to test or measure? Obviously one does not use a ruler to measure weight or a bathroom scale to measure length, but the sociologist who is concerned with, say, attitudes toward using school buses to achieve integration or the relation between the type of family in which one grows up and the kind of occupation one chooses must be quite a bit more careful when he asserts that he is indeed measuring the variables contained in his hypothesis. If, for example, I assert (or hypothesize) a relation between amount of education and the tendency to vote for political candidates of "liberal" persuasion—the higher the educational level, the greater the tendency to vote for such candidates—and then select as my subjects professionals who live in suburbs, am I in fact measuring this relation or am I measuring, rather, the

[18] Presented by Louis Wirth in his classes.

impact of income and residence on voting preference (the city Democrat becoming the suburban Republican)?

The sociologist is also concerned about the *reliability* of his research. If that research is repeated, by himself or others, will it yield essentially similar results? We exhibit this concern because we ought not to have to reinvent the wheel every time we begin a study; that is, we ought to be able to say that we have reasonable confidence in the ability of a particular technique to generate data that are expected because such data have been found in the past. Then we can apply or modify the research instrument to suit the demands of the moment and so move from the known to the unknown. Thus, because repeated administration of a test that relates independence of individual judgment about an event to group pressure toward conformity in judgment has demonstrated that a person becomes increasingly reluctant to act independently as more group pressure is applied, we may expect similar results in the future. We can use that expectation as a point of departure for further new study of related matters without having to question the legitimacy of the relation itself.

Finally, the sociologist wonders about the resulting knowledge that will accrue from his investment of time and money. The sociologist is, after all, only human. He is unwilling to spend half his working life waiting for the research pot to boil. To the extent that he is successful, given that investment, to that extent can his work be assumed to be precise.

To reiterate, the sociologist's perspective is neither strange nor incomprehensible but depends on the questions the sociologist asks with respect to both his conception of the field and the conduct of his investigations. This perspective stems, further, from the terms (and thus the analytical categories) used by the sociologist to order and interpret what he sees. Sociologists have experienced difficulty in developing a clear and unambiguous vocabulary because so many of the words they would want to use are those of everyday speech and carry the emotional overtones of their conventional usage. Really, how does "the *crowd* on the corner" differ from "the *crowd* I hang around with" or "the *bunch* of guys" or "that old *gang* of mine"? The differences among these terms lie in the connotations we bring to each. However, science must use terms that are not only precise in what they define and what they differentiate but also general in that they include all the members of the class of phenomena being defined. Sociologists are not interested in this crowd or that crowd or even in the description of crowds at any particular time. Rather, they see crowds as a special kind of social relationship, making for special kinds of behavior that are different from the behavior that takes place in other social aggregations. As various kinds of crowds come into being, the sociologist must be able to categorize them, too. This attempt at linguistic precision should not be looked upon as pedantry, the joy some may feel in constructing words or special ways of using conventional speech for its own sake (although, to be sure, some sociologists, it is charged, seem to derive pleasure from doing exactly that).[19] Without common responses, without a universe of discourse, communication of any sort becomes impossible. Such a common understanding of symbols is especially required of a science, where every act depends on absolute clarity of interpretation. Sulphuric acid is H_2SO_4 in France, Czechoslovakia, the United States, or Israel. Consequently, to the chemist the implications of $Ca_3(PO_4)_2 + 3(H_2SO_4) \rightarrow 3(CaSO_4) + 2(H_3PO_4)$ are clearly understood wherever he may live and work, even though you and I may be able to make no sense of it whatever.

But, you may wonder, why all this discussion about sci-

---

[19] See the review of Talcott Parsons's *The Social System* by Ellsworth Faris in *American Sociological Review* 18 (February, 1953): 103–6.

ence? Why belabor the point that sociology is a science? Is my insistence on the point an ego trip for me and a put-on for you? This is a legitimate question, and it requires an answer—not solely for clarification of what has been said but also as a prelude to additional discussion.

Both the subject matter of the field and its history have suggested to many observers that the search for a science of society is futile, that such a search at best will produce "social studies," a kind of civics course writ large. And it is true that much of what passes for the scientific analysis of social behavior is no more than name-calling or the attempt to assign blame or responsibility for the existence of some social problem or presumed evil. What is responsible for increases (or declines) in narcotics use? in the deterioration of city centers? in premarital sexual relations? However necessary such assessment might be on occasion, the hurling of epithet or invective is no substitute for the dispassionate acquisition of knowledge. But being dispassionate in observing the human scene is not easy. It is much easier to say that this should be, that should not—especially when so much of the world about us cries out for reshaping, for the recognition once again of man's humanity, which is so often denied. Growing up in a housing project or a ghetto tenement is a very different experience from growing up on a tree-lined street on the exurban fringe. Death in Harlem or Watts may be very different from death in Grosse Pointe or Beverly Hills. The problems of the battered child, the maimed veteran, the man retired too early as obsolete all require constructive action. Group against group, faction against faction. So, sociologist, where are *your* solutions?

Honestly, I have none. I would argue that, by virtue of his training, as well (perhaps) as of the very motivation that brought him into the field in the first place, a sociologist can approach human problems only from the perspective of a pervasive commitment to the maintenance and enhancement of the integrity and personal worth of every human being through the development of precise, reliable, and valid knowledge about human social behavior. Most sociologists, I think, recognize that every person is bound up with every other, that the fate of one is indissolubly linked with the fate of others. Therefore, to the degree that any man denies to another the right to grow, to dream, to live with dignity, he will ultimately deny these rights to himself. John Donne said, "No man is an island." He was right. I firmly believe that the more knowledge we have of human interaction, the better equipped all of us will be to cope with that common fate and possibly to build a common future.

However, having said this, I must add that most sociologists would assert just as firmly that when gathering knowledge as sociologists (as distinct from such actions as they may take directly as concerned citizens) they have the parallel obligation not to let their commitments intrude on scholarship as well as to make their biases explicit so that their work may be judged by others in full awareness of the platform of values on which it stands. In other words, the sociologist may wish to serve the human cause by using knowledge to expand the human potential. But as he gathers the information that might help him to so serve, he has no right to inflict his personal biases, wave his own flag, under the guise of rational, unprejudiced discourse. All sociologists have going for them is the knowledge they have gathered. They hope that this knowledge, when appropriately used by those in the helping professions, government, business, will serve the cause of man. But from the point of view of the sociologist, should he feel that his findings are ill-used, as professional and as citizen he has the right, indeed the obligation, to speak out in protest. If, for example, the reports of a sociological investigation of black-white interaction in a public housing unit are used as data by those who would abolish such housing, the sociologist ought to speak out. Should the sociologist be asked to gather data to "prove" a point, he has a professional obligation to refuse. Thus, Latin American sociologists bridled when they found that some of their American colleagues were employed by an agency of the U.S. Government to develop information on the possibilities of revolution in South America. This, said the sociologists from South America, smacked of imperialism and was a perversion of scholarship. Amid a flurry of publicity, Project Camelot came to a quick and embarrassing end.[20]

It must be admitted nevertheless that this view is not shared by all practicing sociologists. There are many, particularly the younger members of the profession, who argue that the plight of blacks, women, members of the Third World, and the poor demands solutions now.[21] If one is committed to making constructive contributions to his fellow man, the very expertise of the sociologist insists that he stand up and be counted. Certainly, the dispossessed cannot be expected to wait patiently while someone cloistered in an ivory tower spends years analyzing reams of computer printouts to discover that the disadvantaged are disadvantaged.

In addition, many sociologists, including some not so young, assert that they too are exploited, as they are compelled to play it the company way—that the pressure to survive through publication and the procurement of funds for research makes the sociologist, who really ought to know better, as much an organization man as anyone employed by IBM or the Bell System. As a result, it is claimed, the sociologist often prostitutes himself. Knowledge becomes what the granting agency or the periodical wants to see.[22]

[20] Irving Louis Horowitz, ed., *The Rise and Fall of Project Camelot* (Cambridge, Mass.: MIT Press, 1967).

[21] See Carol Brown, "From the Washroom," *American Sociologist* 4 (May, 1969): 158; Martin Nicolaus, "Remarks at ASA Convention," *American Sociologist* 4 (May, 1969): 154–56; and Andrew J. Weigert, "The Immoral Rhetoric of Scientific Sociology," *American Sociologist* 5 (May, 1970): 111–19.

[22] Everett C. Hughes, *Men and Their Work* (Glencoe, Ill.: Free Press, 1958), pp. 157–75.

Therefore, I have discussed the application of the scientific image to sociology to suggest to you that change, betterment, the redress of long-standing grievances will not come about by a call to arms or by manning even the intellectual barricades. I believe that change will come only through single-minded dedication to the generation of verified knowledge, which can become the basis for change.

Yet this view too has its dangers. Too often, as sociologists compile their data and proclaim that they are scientists, the individuals who are at the basis of their results—real live people—get lost in the shuffle. Sometimes there is little congruence between research reports and the aspirations and integrity of those who are too often seen as no more than "subjects." Sometimes even the best-intentioned of sociologists becomes so enamored of what Krutch has called "defining the indefinable and measuring the unmeasurable" of daily human existence that he sometimes fails to understand those he observes or is insensitive to them, particularly if there are cultural differences between the observer and the observed. Science becomes a fetish to be worshiped and an end in itself rather than a way of knowing.[23]

The sociologist must be a humanist as well as a scientist. If he is to practice his craft with distinction and elegance, he must have what the theologian-physician Albert Schweitzer called a "reverence for life." He must be capable of empathy, of understanding. (In fact, one of the most influential scholars in the history of the field, the German Max Weber, referred to sociology as *die verstehende Soziologie*—"understanding sociology.") This requires, I would submit, that a sociologist must himself love life, that he should be excited and fascinated by all he sees about him, that he should regard all the inconsistencies in human behavior, all the varieties of people one sees, as things to be treasured. He ought to

---

[23] See Lee Braude, "Ethical Neutrality and the Perspective of the Sociologist," *Sociological Quarterly* 5 (Autumn, 1964): 396–99.

be capable of love, in a sense that goes far beyond racing hormones or soft-lights-sweet-music-and-you. Some time ago, in this context, I came upon a passage in *The Firmament of Time* by the anthropologist Loren Eiseley. It so impressed me that it has become my own personal credo; I include it here because it expresses so clearly the sort of person the sociologist should be and what, perhaps, sociology—indeed, education in general—might help us all to become.

Man on the inside is quick to accept scientific judgments and make use of them. He is conditioned to do this. This new judgment is an easy one; it deadens man's concern for himself. . . . We wait for the next age to be brought to us by Madison Avenue and General Motors. We do not prepare to go there by means of the good inner life. We wait, and in the meantime it slowly becomes easier to mistake longer cars or brighter lights for progress. And yet—

Forty thousand years ago in the bleak uplands of southwestern Asia, a man, a Neanderthal man, once labeled by the Darwinian proponents of struggle as a ferocious ancestral beast—a man whose face might cause you some slight uneasiness if he sat beside you—a man of this sort existed with a fearful body handicap in that ice-age world. He had lost an arm. But still he lived and was cared for. Somebody, some group of human things, in a hard, violent and stony world, loved this maimed creature enough to cherish him.

And looking so, across the centuries and the millennia, toward the animal men of the past, one can see a faint light, like a patch of sunlight moving over the dark shadows on a forest floor. It shifts and widens, it winks out, it comes again, but it persists. It is the human spirit, the human soul, however transient, however faulty men may claim it to be. In its coming man had no part. It merely came, that curious light, and man, the animal, sought to be something that no animal had been before. Cruel he might be, vengeful he might be, but there had entered into his nature a curious, wistful gentleness and courage. It seemed to have little to do with survival, for such men died over and over. They did not value life compared to what they saw in themselves—that strange inner light which has come from no man knows where, and which was not made by us. It has followed us all the way from the age of ice, from the dark borders of the ancient forest into which our footprints vanish. It is in this that [some have] glimpsed the eternal, the way of the heart, the way of love which is not of today, but is of the whole journey and may lead us at last to the end. . . . For man may grow until he towers to the skies, but without this light he is nothing, and his place is nothing. Even as we try to deny the light, we know that it has made us, and what we are without it remains meaningless.

We have come a long road up from the darkness, and it well may be—so brief, even so, is the human story—that viewed in the light of history we are still uncouth barbarians. We are potential love animals, wrenching and floundering in our larval envelopes, trying to fling off the bestial past. Like children or savages, we have delighted ourselves with technics. We have thought they alone might free us. . . . [O]nce launched on this road, there is no retreat. The whirlpool [of change so rapid as to bewilder and threaten] can be conquered, but only by placing it in proper perspective. As it grows, we must learn to cultivate that which must never be permitted to enter the maelstrom—ourselves. We must never accept utility as the sole reason for education. If all knowledge is of the outside, if none is turned inward, if self-awareness fades into the blind acquiescence of the mass man, then the personal responsibility by which democracy lives will fade also.

Schoolrooms are not and should not be the place where man learns only scientific techniques. They are the place where selfhood, what has been called the "supreme instrument of knowledge," is created. Only such deep inner knowledge truly expands horizons and makes use of technology, not for power, but for human happiness. As the capacity for self-awareness is intensified, so will return that sense of personal responsibility which has been well-nigh lost in the eager yearning for aggrandizement of the asphalt man . . . by our concentration upon material enjoyment and our expressed contempt for the man who thinks, to our mind, unnecessarily.

Let it be admitted that the world's problems are many and wearing, and that the whirlpool runs fast. If we are to build a stable cultural structure above that which threatens to engulf us by changing our lives more rapidly than we can adjust our habits, it will only be by flinging over the torrent a structure as taut and flexible as a spider's web, a human society deeply self-conscious and undeceived by the waters that race beneath it, a society more literate, more appreciative of human worth than any society that has previously existed. That is the sole prescription, not for survival—which is meaningless —but for a society worthy to survive. It should be, in the end, a society more interested in the cultivation of noble minds than in change. . . . Only when man has recognized this . . . will science become . . . something . . . "touching upon hope." Only then will man become truly human.[24]

[24] From *The Firmament of Time* by Loren Eiseley. Copyright © 1960 by Loren Eiseley. Copyright © 1960 by The Trustees of the University of Pennsylvania. Reprinted by permission of Atheneum Publishers.

In such a view, then, sociology becomes not only a search for greater insight into the human condition through the study of recurrent interaction. In addition, the field of sociology may serve as a vehicle by which one might cope with his world, by becoming more personally aware, through the application of a sociological perspective to one's own behavior. This is not to suggest that sociology is by any stretch of the imagination anything like a religion, or that it can provide a philosophy of life or even a design for living. What a person may do as the result of such an examination depends upon his own definition of his situation. As the folk song puts it, "You've got to cross that lonesome valley all by yourself; no one else can do it for you." Not even the sociologist.

Therefore, do not ask too much of this field. It is not social therapy. It presents no program to change the world. All the sociological knowledge that may ever be unearthed will be of no good whatever, except of course to other sociologists, unless it is used by those who are in positions to effect change. All the sociologist can do is, by prodding his consumers long enough and hard enough, generate an ideological climate that is receptive to change.

Nor is sociology a form of personal therapy; have no illusions about *that*. Sociologists are no better at achieving meaningful interpersonal relationships than are nonsociologists. The sociologist may not be able to heal interpersonal ills, whether his own or those of others, any better than the nonsociologist can, but at least he has some documentary evidence to suggest what might be wrong. In this there is hope. And hope is what keeps all of us going.

2

Sociology Evolving:
The Roots of a Discipline

MAN'S RELATION to his fellows has been a continuing concern throughout history. Sociology simply represents a contemporary response to that concern. Discussion within a framework labeled "sociological" began in Europe in about 1840 and in North America in the closing years of the last century. Most sociological research is no older than fifty years. So, viewed in a historical context, sociology came upon the intellectual scene only recently.

But sociology is contemporary in another sense as well. Sociology could not have developed without a particular climate of thought to nurture it. The framework of this climate is constructed out of what Weber called the "disenchantment of the world."[1] We have pointed out that, in order to study

[1] Max Weber, "Science as a Vocation," in H. H. Gerth and C. Wright Mills, ed. and trans., *From Max Weber: Essays in Sociology* (London and New York: Oxford University Press, 1946), p. 155. This essay represents the classic statement of the position that sociological inquiry—indeed, scholarship in general—must be ethically neutral. (See also page 51 in the same volume.)

any subject scientifically, one must be dispassionate or detached about it. Before sociologists could begin their work, then, man had to be "demythologized," stripped of the romantic or at least nonrational aura that had surrounded him for centuries. It could be—and has been—argued that in the process Western man became alienated from eternal and unchanging "first principles" (God, for example), which alone could give his life some stability and meaning in a world of ever increasing uncertainty. Perhaps he even became alienated from himself as, Daedalus-like, he strove to reach the sun of complete self-knowledge and was punished for his impetuosity by the continual frustration of partial insight. Be that as it may, the observation still holds that in order to flourish sociology required a contemporary, secular orientation and that without the rationality implicit in secularism, without the willingness to subject experience to empirical verification, sociology would be no more than the dream of a few.[2]

It should be readily apparent that neither this rational attitude nor the sociology that followed from it developed quickly. Both are the outcomes of centuries of speculation. It is the thesis of this chapter that one cannot understand the work of today's sociologists without some sense of that long, slow process by which sociology took root. As each of us is a product of our past, so is knowledge; a more realistic picture of the present may be gained when viewed with reference to the past, whether that past is the history of men or of ideas.[3]

[2] See Crane Brinton, *Ideas and Men* (New York: Prentice-Hall, 1950).

[3] On the development of social thought and sociology, see, for example, Howard Becker and Harry Elmer Barnes, *Social Thought from Lore to Science*, 2d ed., 2 vols. (Washington, D.C.: Harren Press, 1952); Emory S. Bogardus, *The Development of Social Thought*, 3rd ed. (New York: Longmans, Green, 1955); Rollin Chambliss, *Social Thought from Hammurabi to Comte* (New York: Henry Holt, 1954); John H. Hallowell, *Main Currents in Modern Political Thought* (New York: Henry

Perhaps the oldest reflection within the Western intellectual tradition about men in groups is found in the Judaeo-Christian religious heritage. Man was created by God to have dominion over the rest of the Divine handiwork. Only slightly lower than the angels, man has the spark of the Divine in him, enabling him to know good from evil and to choose good. Since he is on earth for the greater good and glory of his Maker, his relations with other men are really ethical relations, for, as in the tale of Cain and Abel, to do harm to one's neighbor is to do violence to God. But man does in fact seek to assert his individuality, violates God's ordinance by eating from the tree of knowledge—in an attempt to be greater than God—and is punished for his indiscretion and his arrogance. Now man must die, must bring forth new men in pain, and must even work in a world that is hardly Paradise. Yet hard as his lot may be, redemption is still possible through the acceptance of the gospel (good news) of the atoning sacrifice of Jesus, the God-man, at Calvary. Men are children of God, doing His will on earth, and behaving as He would want them to behave as they work to transform this world into the Kingdom of God.

Still another approach, scarcely less venerable, is that of Greek thought. Man has been placed on earth as the result of the same knowable, natural forces that have placed the trees or rocks on the planet or the stars in their galaxies. Man can be understood as part of the orderly operation of the universe, and the logic and rationality that can discover the action of levers or the motion of the planets can be put to uncovering the actions of men. But what differentiates men

Holt, 1950); Floyd N. House, *The Development of Sociology* (New York: McGraw-Hill, 1936); Don Martindale, *The Nature and Types of Sociological Theory* (Boston: Houghton Mifflin, 1960), pp. 3–97; and George H. Sabine, *A History of Political Theory*, rev. ed. (New York: Henry Holt, 1950). For selections from some of the writers to be discussed in this chapter, see Robert Bierstedt, ed., *The Making of Society* (New York: Modern Library, 1959).

from rocks or trees or even other animals is their inherent sociability. According to Aristotle, man is *zoon politikon,* a social animal. Men can band together in a political compact to achieve desired ends. Whoever is unwilling or unable to do this is not human; he is either a beast or a god.

While the religious tradition viewed all men as equal in the sight of God, Greek philosophers, for all their devotion to the rationality of the intellect, could not see human equality. Men differed in their inborn capabilities; the accidents of birth added constraints. There are men who are born to be slaves, said Plato, and there are men who are born to lead. Each must be conditioned to accept his place in the scheme of things. The most important task of any man is to cultivate the mind, and he who must labor has no time for that. Our words "school" and "scholar" come from the Greek *scholé,* which means "leisure," with the implication that education is a leisure-time pursuit. Anyone who must occupy himself with the daily tasks of survival cannot possibly learn, nor can he lead. So, for the Greeks, all men may have a common sociability, but it is their differences that create the possibilities for a social life. Each contributes whatever he can to make a viable social structure, but that structure, in the last analysis, rests on inequality.

The age of these approaches, the Judaeo-Christian and the Greek, should not belie their current, albeit attenuated, viability. Some say that God is very much alive and that as His children we must build our lives in love and faith and trust. We still endow interpersonal relationships with an ethical component; we seek those that are meaningful, fulfilling, enriching, or simply "good." Until shown otherwise, we assume that people are honest and trustworthy, and we want to welcome others in as straightforward and openhanded a fashion as possible. But others argue, as the classic Greeks did, that the only characteristic men share is the fact of their common biological origin. Otherwise, they differ in their attributes,

their ability to profit from and contribute to their surroundings, and their destinies in this world and beyond. Some of
us entertain the possibility, perhaps never explicitly stated,
that differences in upbringing or education or skin color are
more than skin deep; they are basic and they determine the
way we respond to others—the way we maintain what has
been called our "social distance." The dialogue between
these perspectives currently appears as an insistent counter-
poise to more reasoned attempts to make some sense of the
human condition.

But for some eighteen hundred years these two views constituted far more than an undercurrent to speculation. On the
contrary, the religious and the Greek approaches to man in
society constituted the very fabric of inquiry about that subject (and, as we shall see, the tearing of that fabric was
necessary before sociology could emerge) from the time of
Christ to virtually our own day. That fabric was essentially
political. Neither Greek nor Christian scholars could conceive of man outside the political commonwealth. The major difference in interpretation lay in the source of authority
of this state. Either the state was subject to the hegemony of
reason applied by the intellectually astute, or the state owed
its allegiance to the immutable laws of God as interpreted by
His holy Church (which, of course, was right reason well
applied, as Saint Thomas Aquinas put it). However, with
the decline of the Greek view as a *conscious* persuasion in
the first few centuries after Christ and the corresponding
triumph of the Church, particularly after the Council of Ni-
caea in A.D. 325, both the state and man within and inseparable from it came increasingly to be viewed as a religious
community.

In his definition of this community, the medieval thinker
frequently drew an analogy between the organization of the
biological organism and that of the social organism, or state.
Both were created by God in His wisdom. Each organ of the

physiological body—arms, head, heart—has its task, as does each organ of the political body (even today we use the term "body politic"): rulers, clergy, soldiers, tillers of the soil, artisans. From this perspective, it is heresy to tamper with an organism. Consequently, the maintenance of the stability of the organism becomes of paramount importance. Each individual and group should recognize its place, contribute to the well-being of the whole, and eliminate the advocates of change. Change leads not merely to disequilibrium but to damnation.

But there were new currents of thought abroad. The year 1000 dawned. There was no apocalypse; the Christ did not return in glory as had been foretold. Multitudes wondered at the unfulfilled prophecy, and Peter the Hermit found the obvious answer. How could there be a new Jerusalem when the old was in the hands of the infidel? Only a crusade could bring the millennium and win back the Holy Land for God's greater glory, thus validating scriptural predictions. Thousands took up the cry and, again and again, old men and children traveled across Europe and into Asia Minor to do battle with the heathen, pillaging, plundering, and proselytizing along the way in the name and to the honor of God. It was as if the personal example of the crusader could literally will the dawn of a new age.

Although Palestine was not, by and large, recovered for the Cross, the seeds of destruction of medieval civilization were sown in those struggles. The Christian peasants who were freed from their serfdom in general papal amnesties saw the heathen Muslim living in far better conditions than they. Christian thinkers encountered in this contact of cultures the far more cosmopolitan Arabic philosophy. It could be argued that out of such ferment emerged a skeptical spirit, which led eventually to the kind of science we take for granted today, to the Reformation, and, for our purposes, to sociology.

The developing climate of rationalism, the willingness to subject phenomena to sensory verification, provided the necessary impetus for the gradual emergence of a philosophy of the state shorn of a religious overlay. The rise of a bourgeoisie not tied to land for its wealth and the growth of nationalism were changes of such magnitude as to alter European social structure so fundamentally that the stability of former years could never be restored. New justifications for the place of man were required. In the thought of Machiavelli, one senses the origins of a new approach to human relations, still firmly in the tradition of tying these relations to the political order but at the same time a world away in its analysis of the linkage.

Sixteenth-century Europe was an arena for political intrigue of the most intense sort. The continent consisted of a large number of states ruled by princes at various levels of nobility. Each of them jealously guarded his particular plot of land and claimed for himself a freedom of life and action largely unencumbered by the laws of man or church. If one of these petty rulers wished to exterminate an enemy—and of course there were many, real or imagined—there was a seemingly endless number of techniques available to him, from downright murder with a sword or by choking or poisoning to seduction. No act was too brutal in the struggle for survival of self and kingdom. The mighty of Europe knew these methods and used them. And a Florentine statesman, Niccolò Machiavelli, who had himself waged and almost lost his own fight to survive, wondered from a place of exile whether there was perhaps a less violent strategy to ensure self-preservation.

Partly as an intellectual exercise to while away the tedium of inaction and partly as a way of ingratiating himself with the new ruler of Florence, Lorenzo ("the Magnificent") de Medici—which, incidentally, he was unable to do—Machiavelli wrote in 1513 a kind of manual of one-upmanship for the ruler. *The Prince* sets forth his plan for survival—not in the abstract, but as a practical guide for princely conduct. The principle that underlies the work is simple: it makes no difference how one rules as long as one is able to keep on doing so. If this requires killing, well and good. But if a lie will work as well, then lie. Or cheat, if necessary. If all is fair in love and war, so also is it in the fine art of politics. Promise the people what they want to hear and they will love you— this is the maxim. And if they love you, no earthly power can topple you or your kingdom.

What is interesting for our purposes here, of course, is not so much what Machiavelli advised but the way in which he reached his conclusions. He engaged in the same kind of research that confronts you when a term paper or report is assigned. Obviously, you go to the library. So did Machiavelli. He went back to all the historical records that were available to him in the great libraries of Florence to discover how rulers in the past had been able to survive and make do with what they had. At this time in intellectual history the willingness to undertake research represented a significant shift in the orientation of the thinker toward human behavior. It suggested that understanding could be achieved outside a framework of faith and established tradition. Apparently man could be studied on his own terms, albeit still within a political context. Equally important was the fact that the comparisons and contrasts Machiavelli was able to make in the course of his research permitted him to develop general statements *inductively*, in the fashion of the scientist, rather than to work *deductively* from the general situation to the individual case, as might the philosopher.

Strangely enough, at approximately the same time, Thomas More in England was attempting to develop a model for an ideal state based on Christian principles. He, too, went back to history and synthesized what appeared to be known about the actual political conduct of people who had once been alive. Thus, his *Utopia* and Machiavelli's *Prince,* although composed for very different purposes, both demonstrate the beginnings of a drive toward objectivity as political theory slowly divested itself of a rationale for behavior couched in the language of religion. Regardless of the moral that would be drawn, behavior itself was treated as the basic datum of experience.

Once political theory was divorced from a theological stance and it became possible to treat human conduct from a secular point of view, the next logical step leading to sociology was the attempt to separate statements about political behavior from statements about human behavior in general. This shift in interest from political theory to social theory appears to have been attempted first by an obscure Neapolitan, Giovanni Battista Vico (1668–1744). Although he wrote a great deal, his fame rests on one book, *La scienza nuova (The New Science),* published in 1725. Vico wished to construct a "new science" of man. This had never been tried before, he said, because people had labored under the false assumption that a knowledge of man was unattainable because of his God-derived, and therefore God-like, nature. Rather, Vico argued, it is the physical world and its laws that are accessible to God alone. In contrast, *we* obtain our knowledge of the social world from our direct participation in it.

This fact suggested two things to Vico. First, the affairs of men are subject to natural laws, hence divine intervention through miracles has no place in directing human activity. These natural laws of social life can be discovered through the comparative analysis of cultures. What can we learn of the "laws" of family life, for example, by studying families in different times and places?

Second, our ability to become involved in a common human enterprise is indicative of a common human nature. Human nature is constant throughout history, while culture— the customs, traditions, and habits of a people—changes ever so slowly. All nations pass through unending cycles of transformation, from the primitive to grandeur to decadence; this *corso-ricorso* is the fundamental law of man. As we compare cultures and see their parallel development (when abstracted from the temporal sequence of particular events), we are able to predict what changes will occur to a nation (or people) because, in essence, they have happened at least somewhere in the world before. This principle provides us with the key to comprehension of the human condition and, however devout we may be, places that interpretation firmly within a secular framework. Real insight will come when, given an awareness of the interplay between culture and human nature, the human intellect will be able to fathom these laws of sociability, set them down, and use them to anticipate and possibly direct the course of change among peoples and of history in general. With this, social science became possible, for after Vico the split between social and political theory was irrevocable. An increasingly naturalistic world view had taken from man his supernatural cast; he had become "natural," to be viewed with the same detachment as one might use to examine the rest of the world about him, since one could now study man scientifically.

The stage was now crowded with individuals who in one way or another took it upon themselves to provide the kind of knowledge Vico suggested was necessary. Such a person was the Baron de Montesquieu (1689–1755). The thesis of his book *The Spirit of the Laws* is that every nation has a particular "spirit," which is both psychological and sociocultural, comprising artifacts, ideology, social structure. Montesquieu suggests that the laws of nations ought to reflect and be in accord with their guiding spirits in order that the form of government might be effective and relevant for a specific group living in a specific place at a particular time. To put this in another way, government derives from the ways of behaving, believing, and thinking characteristic of a people. What is "good" government for one group is not necessarily appropriate to another, nor, for that matter, need it continue to be "good" over time.

This moral and social ethos, this "spirit," does not occur by chance, says Montesquieu. Geography, climate, forms of trade and systems of currency, population trends, religious convictions all play a part in the development of the general sentiment. But, it is important to note, these influences themselves do not operate randomly. It becomes possible to attribute the emergence of a particular national character to the variety and intensity of particular antecedent influences —especially the influence of geographic and climatic forms. This is virtually suggestive of causality and, by inference, of predictability; that is, it becomes possible that, given influences a, b, c, one can suggest the development of a "spirit" (character or ethos or style—call it what you will) A, while with influences a', b', and c', spirit B might occur. Thus there are laws of social life that can be discovered through the analysis and synthesis of available empirical data. Moreover, one can use this knowledge, according to Montesquieu, rationally to suggest a direction in which the behavior of a social group might tend. On one level, of course, Montesquieu might still appear to be an interpreter of the political framework, but a closer examination of his work should indicate that "the nation" serves only as a fiction to provide for a more general consideration of collective life. It is in this vein that *The Spirit of the Laws* may be viewed as a further significant step in making it possible to study human behavior objectively.

Rousseau and Locke and Edmund Burke and Tom Paine. Old orders topple in Europe and America. Declarations setting forth the "rights of man," "independence," appear as if to declare that nothing is sacred any more. Nothing, that is, but man—puny, bumbling, and cantankerous though he may be. Vico and Montesquieu (among others) seem to have freed man to wonder about himself. Out of this ferment of the dissolution of old regimes and the creation of new ones, sociology finally entered the intellectual arena as a discrete area of inquiry. It acquired an existence in the work of Auguste Comte.

When the Frenchmen who stormed the Bastille in 1789 substituted the individualistic motto of "liberty, equality, fraternity" for the monarchist perception that king and state were inseparable—"I [the king] am the state"—they had no doubt that the gifts of freedom did not apply to those who were lately their enemies. Aristocrats and clergy, supposed plotters against "the people," were hunted down and mercilessly eliminated. The guillotine did its ugly work largely unchecked. Comte was unfortunately born, in 1798, to parents who were both devout Catholics and devout royalists, loyalties not calculated to win friends among the newly emancipated populace. Hounded and persecuted, the Comtes eventually gravitated from his birthplace in Montpelier to Paris. As the young and handsome man grew, he, too, came to reject the views of his parents. Eventually, he even came to reject the society he saw about him—even to the point of attempting suicide. For a brief period he became a disciple and collaborator of the social philosopher Saint-Simon, from whom it is said he borrowed much of his own thinking, particularly his conviction that the society he had rejected was not beyond redemption.

Although as early as 1822 he devised "A Plan of the Scientific Operations Necessary for Reorganizing Society" (with a foreword by Saint-Simon), Comte felt such a practical concern to be premature. He believed it was necessary first to develop a broad theoretical base for any sort of social reconstruction that might be attempted. Accordingly, between 1826 and 1842 he worked on his *magnum opus,* a six-volume work running to more than 4,700 pages and entitled *A Course in Positive Philosophy.* In this work he set forth his justification of and program for a new science of society, a science that he called first social physics and later sociology.

Comte's argument, greatly simplified, runs something like this: The world is out of joint; class pits itself against class, children against parents, freedom of belief has led to immorality, civilization seems about to perish. Why? There is simply so much to be known (can you imagine what Comte might say were he alive today?) that some order must be placed upon the intellectual basis of human life before there can be some order in that life. Consequently, Comte proposes to systematize all existing knowledge. The framework for this herculean task is what he calls the "law of the three stages."

All knowledge passes through three stages, or states. The first is the theological or fictitious. Phenomena are explained in terms of the working of supernatural entities. It rains because this is the will of God. A good man dies while evil persons flourish because this, too, is God's decree. The second stage is the metaphysical or abstract stage. Now the explanation shifts to the intervention of abstract forces. Life ceases because one's vital force runs out; light is transmitted by and through a medium called ether, which carries the light corpuscles along. In the third and final stage this explanation, too, is abandoned in favor of the positive or scientific. Here we are to look for sequences of change, causal relationships and concomitant variation. A change in x is attended or accompanied by a change in y. We rely on unbiased investigation carried out with mathematical rigor. Positive knowledge is obviously the best knowledge of all.

The "law of the three stages" generates a second "law" for Comte, the "law of the hierarchy of the sciences." If we exempt mathematics as the tool of all knowledge, an examination of all the fields of knowledge will show, first, that they can be placed on a continuum from "most theological" to "most positive." But the order of placement on the continuum is not fortuitous. The place of one field depends on the place of the others preceding it, because the one contains all the knowledge of the others but advances in precision beyond the others and comes closer to human concerns. Therefore, second, each field "filiates" or descends from those that precede it, in terms of degree of positiveness and comprehensiveness. The order according to Comte looks like this:

astronomy→physics→ chemistry→
biology (physiology)→social physics
↓
psychology

Yes, social physics will be the "queen of the sciences," the most positive of all, because it will utilize the knowledge of all the other fields. It will not need to consider history, nor will it have to defend itself; it will simply generate "laws" of social life, as physics generates laws of the physical world, and will state them dogmatically. This positive science, which Comte eventually came to call sociology (because he discovered that the term "social physics" had already been used by another writer), will aim at an understanding of the social behavior of man in and of itself. For it is only through knowledge that a perfect society can be achieved. Before there can be change there must be some rational basis for deciding what changes there should in fact be. *Savoir pour prevoir;* understand in order to predict. Then it becomes possible to control and direct change, rather than be forever subject to chaotic transformations of social life.

Comte's program for sociology envisioned organized research in two broad areas. The first he called "dynamic sociology"; this would involve studying changes in social systems —revolutions (remember his personal life in the France of his time), fashions, the transformation from the sacred to the secular world, and the like. The second area he called "static sociology"; this would deal with the orderly in social life, the recurring patterns of social relationships that are often referred to today as "institutions"—the family, occupations, schools, for example. In each of these subfields of sociology, the research to be conducted would use mathematics, would aim for inclusiveness or generality, and would attempt to explain social phenomena as simply as possible (the so-called law of parsimony).

Had Comte's concerns stopped with the attempt to develop a new positive science to understand society and thereby change it, all would have been well. Unfortunately, he didn't stop here, and his zeal proved his undoing. Rather, Comte argued that an intellectual transformation of the world in terms of a more "positive" or scientific orientation toward that world was not enough. A moral transformation was necessary as well. Roman Catholicism had outlived its influence because it was simply too emotional to operate effectively in a positive society. Nevertheless, Protestantism wasn't emotional enough, and Judaism was irrelevant, outmoded altogether. What, then, *could* provide the appropriate impetus? Why, sociology, of course. Sociology can become *both* the science and the religion of humanity. If we think about it, is not religion ultimately a human creation? Therefore, one can rationally substitute the human for the divine because the one is the source of the other. So Comte gave us a new trinity. The "Great Being" to be worshiped is man in society. Because the human being lives on earth and, without the bounty afforded by this planet, he is as nothing. Another aspect of the Comtean trinity is the "Grand Fetish," the earth. We cannot ignore the air that we breathe as being absolutely essential to the maintenance of life. The third "person" is therefore the "Great Medium," air. These we shall worship together in temples of sociology, using as holy writ the writings of great men. Sociologists shall be our priests

—or, rather, priestesses. For there is nothing more pure, says Comte, more worthy to be adored, than woman. When sociology triumphs as moral force, "man will kneel to woman and to woman alone."

Comte was able to obtain enough funds to purchase a building in Paris as his "temple of sociology," but his disciples were few. When he died his religion died with him. Not so his new science. Albeit with different orientations, sociology as a distinct field of inquiry gained adherents throughout Europe. As the nineteenth century ended and the twentieth began, expanding interest in sociology in France and Germany was reflected in the emergence of three men whose work, taken together, is responsible for much of the character of contemporary sociology and in whom past and present become one. These three scholars are Emile Durkheim (1857–1917), Georg Simmel (1858–1918), and Max Weber (1864–1920).

Durkheim came first.[4] Operating in the same tradition as Montesquieu and Comte, he, too, wanted a positivist sociology, a sociology that was truly scientific. The science of sociology will earn for itself a place among the social sciences

[4] For material by Durkheim, see *The Division of Labor in Society* (Glencoe, Ill.: Free Press, 1947); *The Elementary Forms of the Religious Life* (Glencoe, Ill.: Free Press, 1947); *Suicide* (Glencoe, Ill.: Free Press, 1951); *The Rules of Sociological Method* (Glencoe, Ill.: Free Press, 1950); *Education and Sociology* (Glencoe, Ill.: Free Press, 1956); and *Professional Ethics and Civic Morals* (London: Routledge & Kegan Paul, 1957). For material about Durkheim, see Harry Alpert, *Emile Durkheim and His Sociology* (New York: Columbia University Press, 1939); Lewis A. Coser, *Masters of Sociological Thought* (New York: Harcourt Brace Jovanovich, 1971), pp. 129–74; Raymond Aron, *Main Currents in Sociological Thought*, 2 vols. (New York: Basic Books, 1967); 2:11–97; Talcott Parsons, *The Structure of Social Action*, 2d ed. (Glencoe, Ill.: Free Press, 1949), pp. 301–470; Robert A. Nisbet, ed., *Emile Durkheim* (Englewood Cliffs, N.J.: Prentice-Hall, 1965); and George Simpson, *Emile Durkheim* (New York: Thomas Y. Crowell, 1963).

when scholars eschew studies of the individual and instead
focus upon the only social realities there are, the social facts.
These social facts constitute all the ways of action that result when people come together. They may assume group
forms—families, churches, political parties—or they may exist
at the symbolic level—language in general or norms, values,
ideologies in particular—but in either case they are expressed
in and through collectivities of individuals. These social facts
exist prior to and apart from any specific individual and,
most important, exert constraint upon the person to act in
those ways which have received group sanction through consensus, or agreement, of the group. In short, the individual
is molded to conform to group standards by his participation
in the group. He shares a common set of symbols, or what
Durkheim called "collective representations," which have
patterns of conforming action built into them; they are social facts at the symbolic plane. Consequently, a group is not
merely a "bunch" of people. It is a moral community with a
common value framework, a common normative structure
which permits group members to see themselves as sharing
a common destiny because they look at the world in the
same way. The extent to which an individual is bound up
with his group determines his individual actions. What we
would normally assume to be intensely individualistic matters, such as religious devotion or the decision to take one's
life, are for Durkheim really group matters.

Therefore, according to Durkheim, the way in which one
must study social phenomena is evident. Social facts must be
studied only in terms of antecedent social facts; the social
cannot be studied with reference to the individual. For example, a person's demeanor at a wedding or at a funeral is
really not a matter of individual volition; he is (presumably)
happy in the former situation and sad in the latter because
he has been "molded" by his group memberships to perceive
(and behave in a fashion specific to) the group demands

made of him in the particular situation. A phenomenon like crying may be "objectively" the same at wedding or funeral, but it is functionally different because of the group definition that has been given to each social setting and the attendant individual perception of it—do we not distinguish between "tears of joy" and of grief? Thus, the essential social fact, and the question to which sociological analysis should be directed, is how social facts exert their influence, the nature of social control in society.

Further, because the group transcends the life of any particular person within it, the behavior engaged in by the widest number of people is to be regarded as the appropriate behavior for the group—for Durkheim the average is the normal—even though it may be morally shocking. In order to discover this generality of behavior we use the statistical study of central tendencies (means, modes). Then the investigator is able to investigate the function of that social fact, that widely practiced behavior, in the life of the group. What need does it serve? What are its implications for order and change in the group? To discover this, the sociologist must ultimately come to grips with the form of the social milieu as the causative agent in determining the collective life of the people within it. To illustrate, crime may be normal for a society at a particular point in its development because it may represent a source of prestige for those who, for one reason or another, lack access to the more traditional routes to prestige. In other words, crime may be widely practiced, even though it may be viewed negatively, because it serves some socially sanctioned, hence socially legitimate, function within the society. It remains for the sociologist to investigate that function and the kind of society in which it may occur. Through such a procedure some semblance of cause may be established, and sociology may thus achieve its goal of predicting from general statements in order to establish more inclusive theoretical propositions.

Now we come to Simmel.[5] Despite apparent differences, he had a good deal in common with Durkheim in that both men were interested in interaction. Simmel was explicit about it: to him, interaction was the central sociological process, and sociology was therefore the study of the forms of sociation which this interaction assumes. Whereas for Durkheim the group was all, the individual was crucial for Simmel. In a sense, these men treat two sides of the same coin. Simmel does not focus on the individual as such but only insofar as he interacts with another or others. Even the single individual is seen in his potential to influence the direction of the group process; his linkage with another forms

[5] For material by Simmel, see Wolff, ed. and trans., *Sociology of Georg Simmel* (n. 17 for Chapter 1); Simmel, *Conflict and the Web of Group Affiliations* (Glencoe, Ill.: Free Press, 1955); "The Problem of Sociology," *Annals of the American Academy of Political and Social Science* 6 (November, 1895): 412–23; "Superiority and Subordination as Subject Matter of Sociology," *American Journal of Sociology* 2 (September, 1896): 167–89, and 2 (November, 1896): 392–415; "A Contribution to the Sociology of Religion," *American Journal of Sociology* 11 (November, 1905): 359–76; "The Sociology of Secrecy and Secret Societies," *American Journal of Sociology* 11 (January, 1906): 441–98; and "How Is Society Possible?" *American Journal of Sociology* 16 (November, 1910): 372–91. For material about Simmel, see, Nicholas J. Spykman, *The Social Theory of Georg Simmel* (Chicago: University of Chicago Press, 1925); Rudolf Heberle, "The Sociology of Georg Simmel: The Forms of Social Interaction," in Harry Elmer Barnes, ed., *An Introduction to the History of Sociology*, abridged ed. (Chicago: University of Chicago Press, 1966), pp. 269–93; Donald N. Levine, ed., *Georg Simmel on Individuality and Social Forms* (Chicago: University of Chicago Press, 1971), pp. ix–lxv (this work contains additional material *by* Simmel but is recommended especially for its introduction); Coser, *Masters of Sociological Thought*, pp. 177–215; and Lewis A. Coser, ed., *Georg Simmel* (Englewood Cliffs, N.J.: Prentice-Hall, 1965). The entire May, 1958, issue of the *American Journal of Sociology* (vol. 63) is devoted to an appraisal of Simmel and Durkheim; see especially, Lewis A. Coser, "Georg Simmel's Style of Work: A Contribution to the Sociology of the Sociologist," pp. 635–40, and "A Contemporary Academic View of Georg Simmel," pp. 640–41. The latter is a letter of evaluation not only of Simmel but of sociology itself, as both were viewed in 1908.

a group, while his departure may destroy it and his introduction into an existing formation may considerably alter it. The group, in short, does not exist apart from the individuals who form it, but, as in Durkheim's view, it may acquire a character quite distinct from its individual components.

Consider the smallest group possible, composed of two people, the "dyad." Whether it be momentary, as when someone asks directions of another in a strange town, or organized for some extended interaction, Simmel suggests that the two who form it come together voluntarily; if one person refuses to interact there can be no group. Moreover, if one of the parties quits the group, the structure ceases. Consequently, a dyad can be very fragile since it depends for its existence on the willingness of both individuals to "stick it out." Further, each individual must carry his share of responsibility; there can be no shifting of responsibility where there is no third person. Sometimes, according to Simmel, the dyad may acquire, as it were, an existence of its own because of the benefits that may accrue to the two individuals just by remaining in it. For example, a partnership permits the pooling of resources and the conduct of business in a manner beneficial to both participants. Now, neither may like the other or even see the other, communication being handled through a third party—a lawyer, let us say. Nevertheless, in this way the conduct of the business is possible. Since by law each partner is legally responsible for the acts of the other, both must acknowledge the dissolution of the group even though only one of the participants may have grown disenchanted.

A group of three, a "triad," presents a quite different picture to an observer precisely because of that third person. He may be attached to an existing dyad voluntarily, as a mediator of a dispute, or he may join a dyad against his will, as in the case of the first child born to a couple. (Most of us, whether firstborn or not, can probably remember responding to parental demands for affection or thanks with some comment like: "Did I ask to be born?") If the dyad is fragile, the triad is more fragile still. Simmel observed, and subsequent research has confirmed his observation, that a triad breaks down into a dyad plus one. (As an example, remember what you did when one parent told you to go to bed earlier than you wished? You went to the other parent, attempting to get the hour of reckoning changed to your advantage, and, in the process, play off one parent against the other. If you were lucky—at least for a while—such manipulation worked until your parents discovered what you were up to and together stood firm. Then you were lost.) And should one of the parties in a triad leave, the group will continue despite his departure.

Simmel argues that when the sociologist studies the "forms of sociation" he is to be concerned solely about their form and not their content. This means that a sociologist interested in middle management would be (Simmel would say) less interested in the company for which middle management works—whether it be the Roman Catholic Church, the Mafia, ITT, Macy's, or a university—than in the fact that a particular style of interaction occurs among persons similarly situated in any organizational hierarchy. Moreover, as the number of people interacting determines the form the interaction takes, the sociologist must be able to relate number and form in order to get a picture of the social reality he studies. As a result, the sociologist will use not only statistical material but also historical data along with his own insights to understand the social and the psychological as well. Simmel's essay on the "mental life" of the metropolis illustrates this: it is not simply large numbers of people that make a city but the cheek-by-jowl interaction at a rapid, almost breathless, pace, coupled with a catholicity of interests and a tolerance for diversity. But, most important, only when sociology can become abstract, when it can divorce the concern with form from content (which can be left to the other, less general, social sciences), can it become the generalizing science it was meant to be.

Granting that we have only scratched the surface, even this cursory treatment might suggest that, where Durkheim dealt with the generalities of social structure, Simmel was concerned about what happens "inside" the structure. Durkheim was interested in the consequences of interaction, while Simmel was the geometer of that interaction. But then there is Max Weber.[6]

Thomas Aquinas called Aristotle "the master of them that know." It would not be stretching a point to think of Weber as the sociologist's Aristotle. No more creative mind can be found in the history of the discipline, no name is more often encountered in sociological discussions, and, it is fair to say, no person in the pantheon of sociologists past or present is

[6] For material by Max Weber, see *General Economic History* (Glencoe, Ill.: Free Press, 1950); *The Protestant Ethic and the Spirit of Capitalism* (New York: Charles Scribner's Sons, 1958); Gerth and Mills, eds., *From Max Weber: Essays in Sociology; The Theory of Social and Economic Organization* (London and New York: Oxford University Press, 1946); *The Methodology of the Social Sciences* (Glencoe, Ill.: Free Press, 1951); *The Religion of China* (Glencoe, Ill.: Free Press, 1951); *The Religion of India* (Glencoe, Ill.: Free Press, 1958); *Ancient Judaism* (Glencoe, Ill.: Free Press, 1951); *The City* (Glencoe, Ill.: Free Press, 1958); *The Sociology of Religion* (Boston: Beacon Press, 1963); and *The Rational and Social Foundations of Music* (Carbondale, Ill.: Southern Illinois University Press, 1958). For material on Weber, see Aron, *Main Currents* 2:179–252; Reinhard Bendix, *Max Weber: An Intellectual Portrait* (Garden City, N.Y.: Doubleday Anchor Books, 1960); Julien Freund, *The Sociology of Max Weber* (New York: Pantheon Books, 1968); Paul Honigsheim, *On Max Weber* (New York: Free Press, 1968); Karl Loewenstein, *Max Weber's Political Ideas in the Perspective of Our Time* (Amherst: University of Massachusetts Press, 1966), pp. 91–104, a brief but beautiful personal recollection of Weber; Parsons, *Structure of Social Action*, pp. 500–694; and Talcott Parsons, "Max Weber's Sociological Analysis of Capitalism and Modern Institutions," in Barnes, ed., *Introduction to History of Sociology*, pp. 244–65.

treated with greater awe. The notion of ethical neutrality is his. So is the very popular idea of charisma, so lately discovered by psychologists and advertising agencies. Weber rounds out our sociological trinity by bringing Durkheim and Simmel together in his approach to the field.

This can be seen in Weber's very definition of sociology: "a science which seeks to meaningfully interpret and thereby ultimately explain causally social conduct in its course and effects." Like Durkheim, Weber was interested in developing causal, if-then statements about social behavior that exists when individuals come together in recurring patterns of interaction. But, like Simmel, he called attention to a level of analysis that Durkheim omitted. Social conduct is shaped by the meanings those involved in the interaction bring to it, the way norms and constraints are *interpreted* by individuals acting in an environment of symbols as they ascribe motives for their own behavior and impute (or assign) motives for the behavior of others involved in the interaction. Consequently, the task of the researcher is to make sense of, or "understand" *(verstehen)*, the meanings and motives that people bring to behavior, for only then can the behavior itself be understood. This requires that the researcher attempt to "get inside" the people he studies. In this Weber is like Simmel.

While Durkheim saw consensus as imposed from outside the person, Weber lodged the consensus in the give-and-take of the interaction process, as did Simmel. At the same time, Weber took Durkheim a step further by arguing that sociologists need not be limited either to analysis of structure *or* to interindividual behavior. Ultimately, both have symbolic roots and both can be understood statistically even though the techniques of study might differ. Weber says that even qualitative facts may be understood quantitatively by noting the intensity of relationship (correlation) between the variables being considered.

In short, actions have consequences, says Weber; this is what being human is all about. Sociologists must therefore be aware both of the process of action and of the intention or end of that action. In so doing the dichotomy between form and content or between structure and process becomes conceptually meaningless, and the power of sociology to explain conduct is heightened.

Weber applied his theoretical observations to the most diverse forms of empirical phenomena—religion, economic behavior, authority, power, the political process, law, bureaucratic impersonality, the city, class and status—and his contributions blazed trails still followed by sociologists today.

This triumvirate of Durkheim and Simmel and Weber is important to an understanding of the historical roots of contemporary sociology, not only because these three have largely given sociology its intellectual character (although, to be sure, emphasis has at one time or another shifted from interpersonal to structural and back again), serving as a kind of mortar to cement the contributions of others, but because they have also influenced the development of the field by the examples of their own lives. Weber wrote that the sociologist should never let his own thought and prejudices sway his research or his conduct in the classroom; this is what he meant by ethical neutrality. Weber said it and he believed it. But he was also an activist. He championed unpopular causes, spoke out against what he considered to be injustice, and was an ardent patriot, serving as administrator of a military hospital in World War I as his contribution to German victory. When that victory proved unattainable, Weber threw himself into the attempt to build a democracy out of the ashes of empire, but he died before his vision of the future could be realized.

Though Simmel was denied the university positions he most wanted because of anti-Semitic bias, he did not confine his sociology to the classroom (perhaps because, on occasion, classrooms were denied him) but spoke to the non-scholar, exhorting him along with those who were university-trained to raise his sociological consciousness. Simmel, too, was intensely loyal to Germany, despite its rebuffs to him, and served as a propagandist during World War I even though he was largely in scholarly retirement.

Durkheim was an educational reformer who saw the principal use of sociology (much as Comte did) as an aid to the moral reconstruction of society through educational innovation and curricular reform. In other words, Simmel and Durkheim and Weber, and especially the last two, did not use sociology as a kind of personal "cop-out," a way of reducing the problems of living to an abstract and utterly meaningless intellectual exercise. In their lives they argued for the reality of personal involvement, for confrontation rather than retreat; it is an approach currently seen as increasingly relevant and appropriate to our own time.

Finally, to complete the eventful history of sociology, the field reached North America in the last decades of the nineteenth century. Courses were offered at Colby College, Columbia University, the universities of Kansas, Michigan, and Wisconsin, and at Stanford University. However, the impetus to development of sociology on this continent came in 1892, when the University of Chicago opened its doors.[7] The new university was built with money provided by the Rockefeller family, and its first president, William Rainey Harper, was given *carte blanche* to recruit the best faculty he could get for the fledgling institution, secure in the knowl-

[7] See Robert E. L. Faris, *Chicago Sociology, 1920–1932* (San Francisco: Chandler, 1967); Albion W. Small, "Fifty Years of Sociology in the United States—1865–1915," *American Journal of Sociology* 21 (May, 1916): 721–864; and Harry Elmer Barnes, "Albion Woodbury Small: Promoter of American Sociology and Expositor of Social Interests," in Barnes, ed., *Introduction to History of Sociology*, pp. 409–35. Small was the first to translate Simmel into English and thus introduced Simmel's thought into American sociology.

edge that a full purse would support his recruiting efforts. And recruit he did; in fact, some universities accused him of the unethical practice of luring scholars with money, much as athletes were lured later. Harper was able to offer full professors the scandalous salary of *seven thousand dollars* per year. Among those he attracted was one Albion Woodbury Small, a theologian and historian turned sociologist (the syllabi for social science courses he offered at Colby College in the mid-1880's are reputed to be the first printed documentation of a sociology course to appear in the United States), who was appointed "head professor of sociology" and charged with building a department. By 1893 there was a department, and by 1895 it had produced its first two doctorates, which were also the first doctorates in sociology ever awarded in the United States. Ultimately the character of the research undertaken in the Department of Sociology at Chicago and the number and quality of the students who passed through its academic program gave that department a dominant position in American sociology which lasted well into the 1950's.

The influence of "Chicago sociology" on the growth of the field can be found, first, in the thoroughgoing dedication of the members of that department and the curriculum they fostered to a sociology shorn of speculation and moralizing. The earliest faculty and those who constituted the "second generation"[8] knew the writings of Durkheim, Weber, and Simmel and were able to integrate the thought of these three individuals into a coherent prospectus for a science of sociology.

That prospectus, put simply, conceived of sociology as an attempt to develop general statements, based on research, about organized human behavior that results from recurring patterns of interaction. In order to accomplish this, the sociologist must acquire some sense of the reciprocal relation

[8] See Faris, *Chicago Sociology*, pp. 26–50 *passim.*

between the collectivity of individuals—the group—and the single individual involved in such a collectivity. And he must view the individual-group linkage against the backdrop of an environment (including other people and groups) with which it interacts and a culture that continually impinges upon that ongoing interaction.

From our vantage point in the mid-1970's, such a program for sociology appears self-evident. But fifty or sixty years ago the desire to implement a "positive" science of sociology as distinct from a concern with ensuring social progress (reform) or muckraking (the sensational exposé of social evils) was in fact a new perspective in American sociology, despite the earlier concerns of Comte. And the people at Chicago developed that program and formulated it clearly and consistently, not only in their expository writings[9] but, even more important, in subsequent research.

That research is in itself remarkable because of its range. One could say that its diversity resulted from the fact that, because sociology was to all intents in its infancy, there was simply more to discover. But an additional essential ingredient of the Chicago approach, which further contributed to its influence, was the view, fostered by Robert E. Park, who taught at the University from 1914 to 1936, that the sociologist ought to exhibit a kind of repertorial curiosity. Whatever happens when people come together should be told. But the story told by the sociologist differs from the story told by the reporter in that the sociologist has a set of analytical categories in which to place that story, to establish relations between events, and therefore need not view any event as unique and, therefore, nonrecurring. So, armed with the conviction that science and "telling it like it is" are

[9] Particularly in Robert E. Park and Ernest W. Burgess, *Introduction to the Science of Sociology* (Chicago: University of Chicago Press, 1921; 2d ed., 1924); and Robert E. Park, Ernest W. Burgess, and Roderick D. McKenzie, *The City* (Chicago: University of Chicago Press, 1925), pp. 1–62.

not incompatible approaches, sociologists at Chicago—students as well as faculty—went out to examine the social life they saw about them. For it was the contention at Chicago that one learns sociology only by doing sociology. And that means, as it were, getting one's hands dirty.

William Isaac Thomas, for example, studied the transformation of peasants from Poland into American city dwellers (1918),[10] and Nels Anderson studied the world of the hobo (1923).[11] Frederic M. Thrasher attempted to apply a sociological stance to the study of gangs in Chicago (1927).[12] Louis Wirth examined the conflict between traditional Jewish culture and an encroaching alien world (1928),[13] while Harvey Zorbaugh studied an entire urban area in which those at the top of the socioeconomic ladder were separated by only a few short city blocks from those at or near the bottom (1929).[14] Everett C. Hughes studied the Chicago Real Estate Board (1928),[15] the dynamics of a French-Canadian town (1943),[16] and the education of medical students (1961).[17] Howard S. Becker studied the role and career

[10] William Isaac Thomas and Florian Znaniecki, *The Polish Peasant in Europe and America*, 5 vols. (Boston: Gorham Press, 1918–21). See also Herbert Blumer, *Critiques of Research in the Social Sciences: An Appraisal of Thomas and Znaniecki's* The Polish Peasant in Europe and America (New York: Social Science Research Council, Bulletin 44, 1939).

[11] Nels Anderson, *The Hobo: The Sociology of the Homeless Man* (Chicago: University of Chicago Press, 1923).

[12] Frederic M. Thrasher, *The Gang* (Chicago: University of Chicago Press, 1927).

[13] Louis Wirth, *The Ghetto* (Chicago: University of Chicago Press, 1928).

[14] Harvey W. Zorbaugh, *The Gold Coast and the Slum* (Chicago: University of Chicago Press, 1929).

[15] Everett C. Hughes, "Personality Types and the Division of Labor," *American Journal of Sociology* 33 (March, 1928): 754–68.

[16] Everett C. Hughes, *French Canada in Transition* (Chicago: University of Chicago Press, 1943).

[17] Howard S. Becker, Blanche Geer, Everett C. Hughes, and Anselm L. Strauss, *Boys in White: Student Culture in Medical School* (Chicago: University of Chicago Press, 1961).

problems of schoolteachers (1952)[18] and the social context of marijuana use (1953).[19] Alfred Lindesmith investigated opiate addiction (1947) and suggested that, from a sociological standpoint at least, narcotics use is not a sickness; the presence of others is required to provide a symbolic framework in which the effects of the presence or absence of the drug can be interpreted.[20] Louis Kriesberg studied perceptions of security and success among retail furriers (1952),[21] Samuel Stouffer and his associates investigated attitudes of the American soldier in World War II (1949–50)[22] in one of the most massive studies ever carried out by American sociologists, and Andrew Greeley examined data on Roman Catholic faculty members in American universities (1973).[23]

Part and parcel of this breadth of interest was the recognition that what the sociologist learned ought to be applicable to the problems and concerns of people. As Park and Burgess put it in their text: "Further advance in the application of social principles to social practice awaits a more thoroughgoing study of the problems [of social life], systematic social research, and an experimental social science."[24] Unfortunately, this view did not persist, either in the Chicago department or in sociology generally (for reasons that

[18] Howard S. Becker, "The Career of the Chicago Public School Teacher," *American Journal of Sociology* 57 (March, 1952): 470–77. See also his "Social-Class Variations in the Teacher-Pupil Relationship," *Journal of Educational Sociology* 25 (April, 1952): 451–65.

[19] Howard S. Becker, "Becoming a Marihuana User," *American Journal of Sociology* 59 (November, 1953): 235–42.

[20] Alfred R. Lindesmith, *Opiate Addiction* (Bloomington, Ind.: Principia Press, 1947).

[21] Louis Kriesberg, "The Retail Furrier: Concepts of Security and Success," *American Journal of Sociology* 57 (March, 1952): 478–85.

[22] Samuel A. Stouffer *et al.*, *The American Soldier in World War II*, 4 vols. (Princeton, N.J.: Princeton University Press, 1949–50).

[23] Andrew M. Greeley, "The 'Religious Factor' and Academic Careers: Another Communication," *American Journal of Sociology* 78 (March, 1973): 1247–55.

[24] Park and Burgess, *Introduction to Science of Sociology*, p. 57.

will be discussed in Chapter 5). But for a long time the idea of a sociology that would be not only scientific but meaningful was manifest in the work of many who were at Chicago, if not in the orientation of the department.

Perhaps the most profound influence of "Chicago sociology" lies in the immediacy of its challenge to generations of sociologists, even those who are, so to speak, just being born as profesisonals. How can the field of sociology, runs the challenge, develop a model of human social behavior that is at once consistent with what can be observed about that behavior and yet provides clues to what has yet to be observed —to structure what we see now and to predict what may yet be seen? The necessity for a science—be it sociology or chemistry—to codify and order knowledge is central to the accumulation of knowledge. The first viable research-based model for ordering the knowledge of sociology was attempted by those associated with the Chicago department. Based on that foundation, the enterprise continues, not only at the University of Chicago but wherever the craft of sociology is taken seriously and seriously practiced.[25]

Whatever sociology may be today, it owes at least some debt to its past. I believe that a knowledge of the past, whether of a discipline like sociology or of a person, provides us with roots which are sorely needed when, in a time of change, little seems permanent or worthy of preservation. A sense of history, I am convinced, counteracts the arrogance that persuades most of us to assume at one time or another

[25] For examples of the ways in which recent and contemporary sociologists of differing perspectives carry on the enterprise of codification consistent with what can actually be observed about human interaction, see C. Wright Mills, *The Sociological Imagination* (London and New York: Oxford University Press, 1959); Talcott Parsons, *The Social System* (Glencoe, Ill.: Free Press, 1961); and George C. Homans, "Social Behavior as Exchange," *American Journal of Sociology* 62 (May, 1958): 597–606.

that the world began just the day before yesterday. Admittedly, the fact that man has been around for a while, dreaming the same dreams as we, making the same mistakes as we, is a sobering thought. But such a context provides a more reasonable framework in which to view who we are and where we might go than the assumption that all is new and untried, just waiting for our genius to bring order out of nothing. The past can provide insights to the present, if we seek them out. This chapter has attempted to provide a brief picture of the past of sociology. We should now be in a more advantageous position to see who sociologists are today. That is the task of the next chapter.

3

The Practice of Sociology

IN THE LAST CHAPTER I tried to indicate that contemporary sociology is a product of centuries of speculation about the social character of human beings. However, sociological inquiry differs from the questions posed by earlier thinkers in that it assumes that social behavior is susceptible to understanding on its own terms, independent of a moral or an ideological framework. The view that men are "sinners in the hands of an angry God" or creatures of the state is very different in orientation from the statement that Americans and Russians may behave differently because of unlike ideological persuasions. Second, sociological inquiry argues the possibility of developing general statements about human conduct since, after subjecting that conduct to rigorous and controlled investigation, interaction is seen to be patterned, repetitive, and hence amenable to prediction. Third, the organization of knowledge so obtained, it is said, can be used to generate new understanding as well as to provide a rational, empirically verified basis for the work of social reconstruction, which advocates of change may undertake.

The answers to the questions sociologists have thus far

asked of the real world have been slow in coming because sociology is still a relatively young discipline and because, as is readily apparent, there is so much to be learned. Moreover, those who attempt to analyze the human scene are, even today, often viewed with suspicion and hostility. Nevertheless, undaunted and incurably optimistic, sociologists pursue their work. This chapter attempts to describe that work and the people who practice it.

There are currently four rather broad areas that seem to define the range of sociological interest.[1]

The area of *theory and method*[2] deals with the logic, strategy, and techniques of sociological analysis, including the application of statistical procedures and methods to that analysis. Although these might appear to be separate and perhaps mutually exclusive concerns, "theory" and "method" are really two sides of the same coin. All scholarly research directs itself both forward and backward in time; it is plugged into an existing body of knowledge, it faces back to what others have done, but it also seeks to reuse and reorder

---

[1] The range of these broad areas may be further illustrated with reference to the list of thirty-five subfields from which members of the American Sociological Association, the professional body of sociologists in the United States (its membership is in fact international), may choose to specify their major areas of competence. These subfields are listed in the appendix at the end of this chapter.

[2] On theory see, for example, George Caspar Homans, "Contemporary Theory in Sociology," in Robert E. L. Faris, ed., *Handbook of Modern Sociology* (Chicago: Rand McNally, 1964), pp. 951–77; Robert K. Merton, *Social Theory and Social Structure*, enlarged ed. (New York: Free Press, 1968), pp. 1–171; Arthur L. Stinchcombe, *Constructing Social Theories* (New York: Harcourt, Brace & World, 1968); and Walter L. Wallace, *The Logic of Science in Sociology* (Chicago: Aldine-Atherton, 1971). Problems in the development of viable sociological theory are suggested by Herbert Blumer, "What Is Wrong with Social Theory?" *American Sociological Review* 19 (February, 1954): 3–10. On method, in addition to the materials cited in Chapter 1, n. 15, above, see John Madge, *The Tools of Social Science* (London: Longmans, 1953).

the knowledge, perhaps in new ways, so as to generate new knowledge and thus move toward or extend the frontiers of inquiry. In order to know *what* to observe we must know *how* to observe. We must know how to structure the environment in order to ask the proper questions of it. This requires a body of interrelated statements about the nature of the territory, pitched at a sufficiently high level of abstraction to show us not merely the territory in question but its relation to other areas. Theory, then, is the intellectual apparatus with which we work to gain a perspective on what we know, or think we know, which would further sensitize us to what is yet to be known.

One could talk about the theory of sociology in general or the theory of one of its subfields—the family, criminal behavior, stratification, or what have you. But in either case the constituents of a theory are the same. First there is a *conceptual scheme*, a set of terms that blocks out a portion of the world and tells us what to see there. Some of these concepts, such as "human being" or "culture," we may accept as givens or we may borrow from other theories; these need not be defined. Others, like "role performance" or "crowd," may need to be defined for the particular theoretical use. Whether they are defined or not, according to George C. Homans, some concepts are *descriptive*, telling us what the subject matter of the theory is: suicide, religious affiliation, upward social mobility. Other concepts, such as intensity, frequency, rate, incidence, are, says Homans, *operative*.[3] They deal with the occurrence or "operation" of the descriptive terms in the real world and are subjected to mathematical manipulation because of their variable quality.

In addition to telling us what to see in that portion of the world in which we happen to be interested, a conceptual scheme serves as a framework in which to place observations

[3] Homans, "Contemporary Theory in Sociology," p. 952.

that have previously been made of presumably relevant phenomena. Once descriptive and operative concepts have been tied together—"as the sun sets, air temperature drops," "political conservatism increases with age"—we have a "fact" or, more explicitly, an "empirical generalization." What I am saying is that what we commonly think of as facts—if x, then y; given a change in x there is a change in y—simply do not exist outside of a conceptual scheme. A "fact" is an outcome of relating observed regularities, and this we cannot do unless we first know what the terms of the relation are. Only when we define do we see.

Now we move up to a higher level of abstraction or idealization. We tie facts, which are themselves relationships, into a *proposition,* which relates the facts as members of a class of objects exhibiting particular characteristics. Thus, suppose we know that "as the sun sets, air temperature drops." Suppose we also know that longer days are associated with hotter temperatures. We are then able to assert the more general proposition that sunlight and air temperature are related. Consequently, a second aspect of a theory is a *set of interrelated propositions,* which tie together more and more empirical generalizations at increasingly abstract levels. The higher the level of abstraction of the theory—that is, the wider its scope—the more useful it is.

How useful should a theory be? I said before that a theory uses what has been learned to suggest where the investigator might venture next in his analysis. Putting this in another way, a theory is useful to the degree that it explains what is already known by more sophisticated or insightful ordering of the data on which the theory is built. That is, as propositions are derived from the "facts" and interrelated, the way in which those propositions are put together is not fixed. The researcher likes to play with his statements to see if there is a greater payoff in understanding those propositions as related in one way as against another. The better the explanation, the greater should be the confidence of the investigator in the approach he has taken to fitting together the propositions.

Which explanation is best depends on the simultaneous ability of a theory to *predict*. Not only must a theory be able to explain what is known about a body of material; it must also be able to generate new knowledge. The better the theory, the more it is able to predict.

So the usefulness of a theory derives not so much from the level of abstraction at which it is pitched as from the degree of explanatory and predictive power it makes available at a given level. Theory 1 may be as wide in scope as Theory 2, but the proof of the theoretical pudding is in what it tells us about existing facts and in the new facts it produces.

A current sociological concern is the extent to which sociological theory, as distinct from a mass of empirical generalizations or low-level propositions, has developed. The controversy is by no means settled, and numbers of sociologists immerse themselves in investigations directed to the development, clarification, and codification of the presuppositions, data, and logic upon which sociological theory could rest. Obviously, most practicing sociologists do not devote their total energies to such endeavors. It should be clear, however, that the initiation of even the most modest empirical study involves some speculation about theory, and the conclusion of that research requires still more speculation in order to relate the results of the study appropriately forward and backward in time. All sociologists, then, theorize at one time or another. There could be no substantive research, nor could the field move forward, even slowly, without theory.

Theory and method are usually treated together because method can be thought of as the objectification of theory. Data do not "just happen." Just as facts are contingent upon a particular theoretical formulation, so data depend on the particular strategy of extraction, which ultimately forces us back to an examination of the underlying theoretical stance of the research.

When sociologists use the term "method" they are really referring to two sorts of enterprises; the specific referent must be inferred from the context of the discussion. More obviously, "method" suggests the techniques and procedures of data collection. However, "method" also refers to the logic by which the collected data are interpreted, inferences drawn, and empirical generalizations asserted. The interrelation of these two enterprises has been well stated by Matilda White Riley:

> Sociological investigators today employ many special empirical methods . . . in seeking new facts and discovering the connections among them. Some conduct controlled experiments in the laboratory; others question cross-section samples of individuals about their opinions and attitudes; still others trace the web of interpersonal attitudes in complex organizations. Some observe and describe small group interaction, while others analyze the volume and density of human populations and the changing rates of marriages, births, and deaths. Some classify and quantify the content of mass communication; others make cross-cultural comparisons of role prescriptions and social structures. Some are concerned with using . . . computers to simulate human behavior. . . .
>
> In each inquiry, the investigator selects, from the common reservoir of these and any other available methods, a particular set of methods that he will follow in obtaining his research findings. This set of selected empirical methods is referred to as the research design.
>
> In making the broad plans for his research design and in choosing the specific technical procedures he will use to carry it out, the investigator decides how he will select certain facts (his data), how he will classify these

facts, and how he will seek to uncover the order or pattern in which they actually occur. . . .

But the researcher rarely concludes the process with . . . specific factual findings, for he also wants to interpret them. Accordingly, having started with theory, he completes the circle in the interpretative phase by bringing the findings back into his conceptual [scheme], setting the new facts into the context of his ideas.

Here the methods that he uses—logical reasoning, mathematics, creative imagination—are less clearly defined. Here there is often no straightforward execution of a clear-cut plan. [But], whatever procedures are used, a major step in the research process is to interpret the empirical data by incorporating them into the more general principles and theories. . . . Indeed (although particular studies often have methodological or applied objectives), the central aim of scientific research, its reason for being, is to add to or test the ideas with which the research began—to extend, revise, specify, confirm or discard [the theoretical orientation that surrounds the specific research].[4]

A subfield of theory and method is *mathematical sociology*,[5] which involves the attempt to apply the concepts and processes of mathematical analysis to the development of quantitative models of behavior. Should this appear to be but an empty intellectual exercise, it must be remembered that it "is the art of science to strip the fullest possible appreciation of events in context down to some core elements deemed essential and then to adhere ruthlessly to the ab-

[4] Matilda White Riley, "Sources and Types of Sociological Data," in Robert E. L. Faris, ed., *Handbook of Modern Sociology*, © 1964 by Rand McNally and Company, Chicago, pp. 978–79, 981–82. Reprinted by permission of Rand McNally College Publishing Company.

[5] See James S. Coleman, *Introduction to Mathematical Sociology* (New York: Free Press, 1964).

straction while matching these core elements with those drawn from other contexts. Mathematics is the most incisive technique for such abstraction and matching."[6] For example, the application of the mathematics of chance to the seemingly unpredictable in social life should make it possible to develop schemes of analysis that inject order and predictability into the explanation of that life. These schemes should have a validity by virtue of their quantitative base that transcends the group being studied and provides a generality of interpretation appropriate to a scientific outlook. Moreover, the use of mathematics permits a kind of "laboratory experimentation" with interacting individuals through the simulation of events by computer without the necessity of having those individuals present and perhaps causing them embarrassment or difficulty. Mathematical sociologists thus view mathematics less as a tool than as an orientation toward things social that can give the social sciences in general and sociology in particular greater control of and explanatory power about the data with which they work and the conceptual schemes that are applied to the data.

A second, and quite varied and extensive, area of sociological interest deals with the study of *social organization and institutions*. Sociologists who practice within this area investigate one or another of the specialized groups that make up society—family, school, church, business concern, and the like—and/or the linkages within and between them that permit the society to function and survive. "Social organization" is a general term that refers to the interrelationships of the total set of social institutions within the society. The institutions themselves are sets of socially sanctioned behavior patterns, which themselves derive from the norms

[6] Harrison White, "Uses of Mathematics in Sociology," in James C. Charlesworth, ed., *Mathematics and the Social Sciences* (Philadelphia: American Academy of Political and Social Science, 1963), p. 78.

and values—expectations of appropriate and desired behavior—operating in the society, which get the "job" of the institution done.[7]

Not all behavior is organized. As Robert Faris points out, some behavior may simply be pluralistic.[8] Many people may flush the toilet at the same time because, watching the same television program, they were simultaneously freed from their servitude by the same commercial interruption. There was presumably little or no interaction between these separate people all doing the same thing at the same time. A good deal of human conduct is of this sort—audience participation, involvement in fads, crowds, riots—and many sociologists are interested in this conduct. But because such behavior is essentially that of individuals in an aggregation and often is without symbolic content, relying on the emotional contagion of nearness (as in a panic on board a sinking ship or in a burning theater), no structure develops, the behavior itself is short-lived, and there are few if any long-term effects on the society.[9]

Sometimes, of course, what begins as pluralistic, unorganized activity may develop a set of norms and expectations, procedures for reaching goals presumably set by the participants, and a differentiation of roles (actions) and statuses (positions) that provides a structure for the management of the goal-oriented activity. The impact on the society and its

[7] Robert E. L. Faris, "The Discipline of Sociology," in Faris, ed., *Handbook*, pp. 1–36; Otis Dudley Duncan, "Social Organization and the Ecosystem," in *ibid.*, pp. 37–82; Everett C. Hughes, "Institutions," in Alfred McC. Lee, ed., *Principles of Sociology* (New York: Barnes & Noble, 1965), pp. 225–66; and W. Richard Scott, ed., *Social Processes and Social Structures* (New York: Holt, Rinehart & Winston, 1970).

[8] Faris, "Discipline of Sociology," p. 7.

[9] See, for example, Herbert Blumer, "Collective Behavior," in Lee, ed., *Principles of Sociology*, pp. 166–222; *idem*, "Collective Behavior," in J. B. Gittler, ed., *Review of Sociology: Analysis of a Decade* (New York: John Wiley & Sons, 1957), pp. 127–58; and Neil J. Smelser, *Theory of Collective Behavior* (New York: Free Press, 1963).

existing organization may be considerable. For example, the increasingly militant demands of women for recognition and autonomy on their own terms that followed upon the publication of Betty Friedan's *The Feminine Mystique* resulted in rallies, boycotts, legal battles, and a variety of other activities by individuals and collectivities, which eventuated in such structures as the National Organization for Women (NOW).[10] And there is certainly no doubt that American life will change markedly, whether in the introduction of women's studies into colleges and universities or in legislation specifying the irrelevance of sex for employment, as a result of the actions of NOW and similar groups. Similarly, the persistence of small Christian groupings in the face of intense persecution in the two centuries following the Crucifixion and their eventual coalescence into the organizationally sophisticated Catholic Church have been of incalculable influence on the course of Western civilization.[11] Thus, some sociologists are fascinated by the transition from unorganization to organization, for in that change is seen the germ of persistent social order.[12]

Of course, many practitioners are interested in the final results—social organization itself. How are authority, power, prestige, influence allocated within a society? What are the paths of movement—mobility—through that social organization? How do the values that operate within it define the activities of the institutional structures within the organiza-

[10] See, for example, the January, 1973, issue of the *American Journal of Sociology*, edited by Joan Huber, which deals with "Changing Women in a Changing Society."

[11] See, for example, Elizabeth K. Nottingham, *Religion: A Sociological View* (New York: Random House, 1971), pp. 227–45; and Talcott Parsons, "Christianity and Modern Industrial Society," in Louis Schneider, ed., *Religion, Culture, and Society* (New York: John Wiley & Sons, 1964), pp. 273–97.

[12] See, for example, Blumer, "Collective Behavior," in Gittler, ed., *Review of Sociology*, pp. 145–51; and Hans Toch, *The Social Psychology of Social Movements* (Indianapolis, Ind.: Bobbs-Merrill, 1965).

tion? That is, how do the values, goals, aspirations of a society make themselves felt in the family or at work? How does this relation between the values of the social organization and the actions of institutions within the organization vary with changes in the prestige or authority level? In other words, are the outlook and behavior of a family whose total income is $3,600 a year different from those of a family whose total income is $360,000 a year? To all these questions you might answer: Obviously. Of course. How trite. Yet there is a good deal of difference between the gut or "common sense" reaction and verified, hard data. Certainly, one does not apply hot cloths to a lump on one's body hoping that it will "go away." Unless the individual wants to gamble with his life, he seeks information that only thorough testing can provide (although, to be sure, the diagnoses based on those tests may differ). So, too, effective action and understanding can come only through knowledge; were policies and programs to be predicated on unsubstantiated assumptions, they would be utterly futile. So we seek to document or validate even the obvious. And sometimes we are surprised to find that the "obvious" is invisible.

Finally, still other sociologists concern themselves with the analysis of a particular institution. Some study work, for example.[13] Since the long arm of the job seems to be always with us, it would seem to be useful to know something about the meaning of work in contemporary society: how people work and how they react to it; how occupations develop, become specialized, or die; the relation between work and leisure and between work and nonwork situations, such as unemployment due to technological obsolescence or to retirement. Some sociologists study the family. The family is of such fundamental importance for the continuity of a social

[13] See Lee Taylor, *Occupational Sociology* (London and New York: Oxford University Press, 1968); and Richard H. Hall, *Occupations and the Social Structure* (Englewood Cliffs, N.J.: Prentice-Hall, 1969).

framework that some anthropologists—Margaret Mead and Ruth Benedict, for example—claim that family form and practice are related to the development of a dominant interpersonal orientation and personality structure in a society. One may not share this view, but it is clear that the family nonetheless profoundly influences the life career of a person, the socialization he receives, and the image of himself he constructs. Consequently, sociologists interested in the family investigate how the family has changed over time, how families differ within and between societies, the problems of family formation and stability—factors influencing the choice of mates, divorce, the planning of family size, and the like—and the influence of the family as structure on those within it, both adults and children. The family represents a unique and ever present laboratory in which a variety of social processes can be examined.[14]

The study of social organization and institutions embraces *applied sociology*, which is to sociology what chemical engineering is to chemistry. Attention is directed to the solution of particular problems posed by some organization rather than to the accumulation of knowledge as an end in itself. To the applied sociologist, the resolution of a problem for a client is central, rather than making the problem serve as a vehicle through which to attack matters of more theoretical interest.

The distinction between "pure" and "applied" research has been subjected to increasing criticism; it is contended that no research can be "pure," for without reference to human concerns scholarship becomes so much idle chatter. What should matter, rather, are the legitimacy of the problem and the integrity of the individual sociologist in dealing with it. In other words, the argument runs, there is nothing wrong in working for some group, and being paid for it, to answer

[14] See, for example, William J. Goode, *The Family* (Englewood Cliffs, N.J.: Prentice-Hall, 1964).

some questions that the group deems important. But the sociologist has the obligation to examine the content of these questions and the uses to which his answers could be put, as in the case of "Project Camelot," discussed earlier. If he feels that he would be ethically compromised by contributing his talents to solving the problems assigned him, he ought not to take the assignment. The scientists who worked on the development of the atomic bomb had similar doubts.[15]

In any case, sociologists who are associated with market or survey research agencies, who operate management-counseling services, or who derive a major portion of their income from consultation on a retainer or fee basis may think of themselves as applied sociologists. In bringing sociology out of the academic building, where it is most frequently found, and into the market place, where sociologist and informed layman can learn from each other, the applied sociologist performs a most useful and needed service.[16]

Comparative sociology[17] proceeds on the assumption that, while the general statements so far developed in sociology appear to be applicable to all societies and throughout history, they have actually derived from research carried on in the highly developed societies of Western culture. The comparative sociologist takes the position that cross-societal comparisons and historical comparisons are essential if sociology is to grow beyond its own cultural boundaries and thus shed the provincialism of an ethnocentric view of human conduct. Comparative sociologists examine the relations among tech-

[15] See, for example, James Phinney Baxter 3rd, *Scientists Against Time* (Boston: Little, Brown, Atlantic Monthly Press, 1946), pp. 426–27; and Lansing Lamont, *Day of Trinity* (New York: Atheneum, 1965), pp. 263–68.

[16] See Alvin W. Gouldner and S. M. Miller, eds., for the Society for the Study of Social Problems, *Applied Sociology: Opportunities and Problems* (New York: Free Press, 1965).

[17] See Robert M. Marsh, *Comparative Sociology* (New York: Harcourt, Brace & World, 1967).

nology, culture, and the interpersonal and structural complexity of societies; kinship; similarities and differences in the value and normative systems of societies; societal evolution; stages of conflict resolution (the achievement of harmony and order); and the like from society to society. They apply sampling procedures and complex statistical techniques to their comparative efforts, along with intensive case studies of societies and cultures. In this analysis, the methods of sociology and anthropology converge so that the boundaries of interest between the two fields appear to break down before a shared body of data and common intellectual concerns.

The *sociology of formal and complex organizations*[18] refers to a body of theory and research directed toward an understanding of the variety of structures that have arisen in our society in order to facilitate the rational accomplishment of an activity defined by some group of people as legitimate or necessary. On the surface, such a definition could refer to any organized group. But what differentiates the structure of "an organization" from some other social structure is that word *rational*. "An organization" proceeds according to *rules* that *formally* define the spheres of action, the authority, and the responsibilities of those who participate in the structure and of those, the clients or customers, who are served by it. Hence organizations are formal; they deal impersonally and dispassionately with a task according to rules of procedure that are theoretically known to all. Problems that affect the ability of the organization to function—a recalcitrant or incompetent employee, for example, or a client who refuses to wait in line to be interviewed—are also handled "by the book," formally. Innovation and idiosyncrasy are discouraged as dysfunctional to the structure. These structures are also *complex*, requiring an extensive network of interconnected statuses both to serve organizational goals and to

[18] See James G. March, ed., *Handbook of Organizations* (Chicago: Rand McNally, 1967).

maintain the integrity and viability of the structure itself. The need to commit actions to paper, rather than rely on word of mouth or memory, gives rise to several layers of support personnel, what C. Wright Mills has called the "enormous file" of anonymous salaried or hourly rated employees, who keep the structure going, who lack real decision-making ability, and, as a result, who are often personally alienated or frustrated.

Sociologists want to know about the way the organization is supposed to work and how it actually does function, the informal communication network of rumor, gossip, and consultation that underlies the formal network outlined in rulebook or table of organization. The sociologist of complex organizations is interested in the ways by which organizations allocate power and rewards, the careers of organization members, the response of the client to the structure. In short, the sociologist seeks to penetrate the impersonal and often forbidding world of "do not fold, bend, spindle, or mutilate" to elicit information about what may well be the most ubiquitous feature of modern life, the bureaucracy.

Industrial sociology[19] represents an expansion of the interests of the sociologist of formal organizations to include the industrial enterprise, whose end product (or reason for being) is the production of goods rather than services. The *sociology of occupations and professions*[20] represents, as it were, the limiting case of these interests, because it deals with the social and structural context of work, whatever the product and wherever that work may be done. The distinction among these three fields of inquiry lies not so much in perspective but in the breadth of data to which the perspective may be applied. Whether the sociologist is interested in work carried on in an organizational context or in industrial

[19] See Delbert C. Miller and William H. Form, *Industrial Sociology* (New York: Harper & Row, 1964).
[20] See n. 13, above.

occupations, or in establishing general statements about work, he will investigate such things as the ways in which people learn work roles, the status and authority structure of the job, the drive for increased prestige of workers *and* occupations, technological obsolescence, the relation between work and leisure, and the problems that accompany status changes at work (promotion, demotion, firing) or disengagement from work altogether (retirement). Taken together, the sociology of formal and complex organizations, the sociology of industry, and, more generally, the sociology of occupations have studied a variety of work roles (caseworkers in a public assistance agency, teachers, federal civil servants, waitresses, dime-a-dance girls, workers on an automobile assembly line, middle management, chiropractors, janitors, morticians, boxers, nurses, shipboard radiomen, rabbis, linotype operators) in a number of settings so that our knowledge of human relations at work has been considerably extended. In the process, much has been learned about social conduct in general.

Social control, it has been said, "is the central fact and the central problem of sociology."[21] As I have suggested, the question of how dissimilar persons are able to achieve concerted action is one of the key questions asked by the sociologist. Because an interest in the modification of conduct as a result of group involvements is so central to sociological study, because this question is a legitimate concern of sociologists, regardless of the group or institution to which they may restrict themselves, the separate existence of this area might seem redundant. Yet the influence of the normative structure on conduct, the importance of ideology, beliefs, myths, rituals, and ceremonies as ways of welding people together, of achieving collective loyalties and reintegrating group identities, cannot be overlooked as subjects of inde-

[21] Park and Burgess, *Introduction to the Science of Sociology* (n. 9 for Chapter 2), p. 42.

pendent study. The ability to see similarities between the hero-worship of adolescent baseball fans and national adulation of a leader, the recognition that professions and religions and nations each have creeds that may inspire similar loyalties—these provide a new perspective on the social ties that bind and the possibility of additional generalizations about human social life.[22]

The *sociology of knowledge and science* examines how groups create and maintain forms of thought and structures of knowledge. Karl Marx proclaimed that the economic organization of a society provided a foundation not only for social life but for the idea systems of that society, that people would perceive themselves and life around them from the standpoint of their relation to the means of production characteristic of their society and to the historical period in which they live. Max Weber, especially in his studies of the relation of religious ideas to social life, sought to reject the Marxian view by suggesting that ideas do not flow from one component of social conduct—in this case the economic—but that religious, philosophic, linguistic, and scientific ideas and values, *together with* the structure assumed by a society, are all interdependent constituents of human action.

It was in the work of Karl Mannheim (1893–1947), notably *Ideology and Utopia*,[23] that this field came into prominence. Mannheim argued that knowledge is a means by which man adapts to his environment, but since the environment is not everywhere the same it cannot be expected that knowledge will be everywhere the same. A particularly important aspect of the environment is the organization of hu-

[22] See MacIver and Page, *Society* (n. 10 for Chapter 1), pp. 136–209.

[23] Karl Mannheim, *Ideology and Utopia* (New York: Harcourt, Brace, 1952); and *idem, Man and Society in an Age of Reconstruction* (London: Routledge & Kegan Paul, 1940). On science see Maurice N. Richter, Jr., *Science as a Cultural Process* (Cambridge: Schenkman, 1972).

mans into groups, especially socio-economic classes. To all intents, therefore, ideas and perceptions and values can be thought to be group-based (especially class-based) as well. Conservative groups might create and maintain a static view of the world, and radical groups might entertain a much more dynamic perspective, while old and young might be in conflict because of their different views of the world and themselves and others in it.

If every group has its own ideology, so that knowledge is related to the perspective of the "knower," Mannheim questions whether any knowledge can be "true" or possess a general validity that transcends the subjectivity of the group. Only the formal, quantified knowledge of the "exact sciences" can cross group boundaries; history and the social sciences must fall short of this desirable universality. Qualitative knowledge (which, according to Mannheim, is largely what is produced by the social sciences) will approach some sort of universality only when scholars from several groups and strata can develop some consensus about what is known and how it is to be interpreted.

To be sure, Mannheim's treatment has been criticized. But his work, along with that of Marx and Weber, has prodded some sociologists to undertake empirical research relating idea systems and values to other social-structural factors. Such matters as, for example, the flow of information about scientific inventions and discoveries, the organization of the scientific enterprise in different countries, the interaction of religion and science, professional socialization, careers in various scholarly fields, and the relation between talent and performance have been studied.

As ideas have increasingly come to be viewed as having social and policy implications, scholarship in this area of sociology has assumed greater urgency. As ideas may flourish and knowledge accumulate in one socio-economic climate, another may inhibit such growth. As knowledge can edify and ennoble, it can also obscure and destroy. The growth of knowledge generated the atomic cloud. It has also led to unparalleled well-being for many and may even lead to peace. Whether to take one road as against another is central to our very survival.

A third broad area of sociological interest is that of *population and ecology*. The study of the characteristics of and changes in the composition of the aggregation of people who make up a given society or territorial unit can tell the sociologist much about trends and changes in a social unit that could not be derived from attitude surveys, questionnaires, or interviews. Knowledge of the growth or decline of a population or of shifts in population from one area of a territory to another (for example, the shift from rural to urban to suburban concentrations of people over the last century) can provide an analytical framework for the understanding of other social changes, such as changes in resource use, in primary school attendance, in concern for older citizens, and the like. The sociologist Louis Wirth suggested as long ago as 1938 that the transition of the United States from a rural to an urban nation has led to a kind of sophistication and worldliness—what he called the "urban way of life"—that will transform the outlook and values of the entire country, rural and urban.[24] It may be that the ability to see what happens in large cities afforded by television, in addition to the ability to hear or read about urban events, has accelerated the process. A leading sociological demographer, Philip M. Hauser, contends that changes in the size, density, and diversity of population are in large measure responsible for what he calls the "chaotic society," a society with many problems and dim prospects.[25] Certainly, the force of population

[24] Louis Wirth, "Urbanism as a Way of Life," *American Journal of Sociology* 44 (July, 1938): 1–24.

[25] Philip M. Hauser, "The Chaotic Society: Product of the Social Morphological Revolution," *American Sociological Review* 34 (February, 1969): 1–19.

itself must be understood in assessing the survival potential of both the individual and the species. Competition for available goods and services is a social problem of great consequence. Its solution disturbed Malthus and Darwin over a century ago and embroils the advocates of "zero population growth" and "right to life" groups today. Sociologists are equally concerned and hope by their research to add reasoned discourse to the conversation.

The study of population (more formally, demography, from the Greek *demos,* "people") has given rise to sophisticated quantitative techniques for the analysis of data, drawn largely from census and other survey material collected by governmental agencies, and for predicting long-term trends on the basis of that analysis. Economists, biologists, and statisticians have made contributions to the measurement of fertility, mortality, and the rate of population change in terms of a variety of socio-economic variables, including ethnic background, education, occupation, and religion.[26]

The study of ecology—and sociologists used the term long before it became popular—places population *and social structure* within a particular territory. The sociologist studies the interaction between that territory and the way a population group distributes itself within it. How do people take what an area has to offer and shape it to their needs? How do successive groups transform the same area as they pass through it? Within a given territory, how do people and groups compete for their own plot of "turf," their own living space necessary to survive? Conversely, how do changes in an area influence particular groups within it? What happens

[26] See, for example, Philip M. Hauser, "Demographic Factors in the Integration of the Negro," in Talcott Parsons and Kenneth B. Clark, eds., *The Negro American* (Boston: Houghton Mifflin, 1966), pp. 71–101; Frank W. Notestein, "Population: The Long View," in Theodore W. Schultz, ed., *Food for the World* (Chicago: University of Chicago Press, 1945), pp. 36–57; and William Petersen, *Population,* 2d ed. (New York: Macmillan, 1969).

when famine or a dust storm or a drought transforms the land?

Virtually since the beginnings of sociology in the United States, much effort has been expended on making some sense of the man-land linkage. Studies of great cities and of the small towns that line both sides of a highway, suddenly giving way to farms or ranchlands, have illuminated American social life, holding the matrix of human conduct clearly up to view. We see people within a spatial context, wrestling with that space to make some sort of meaningful life. The dynamism implicit in such studies has fascinated sociologists and lay persons alike and, I suspect, will continue to do so until survival either appears less precarious or becomes impossible.[27]

The fourth major area of sociological interest is *social psychology.*[28] As its name may suggest, the area is something of a hybrid, for it embodies both sociological and psychological perspectives, is taught in both psychology and sociology departments, and is practiced by both psychologists and sociologists. The mix of the two orientations depends on each

[27] See, for example, Reynolds Farley, "The Changing Distribution of Negroes Within Metropolitan Areas: The Emergence of Black Suburbs," *American Journal of Sociology* 75 (January, 1970, Part I): 512–29; Robert E. Park, Ernest W. Burgess, and Roderick D. McKenzie, *The City* (Chicago: University of Chicago Press, Phoenix Books, 1967); James A. Quinn, *Human Ecology* (New York: Prentice-Hall, 1950); and Gideon Sjoberg, *The Preindustrial City* (New York: Free Press, 1960).

[28] Examples of social-psychological works written from a sociological perspective are Alfred R. Lindesmith and Anselm L. Strauss, *Social Psychology*, 3d ed. (New York: Holt, Rinehart & Winston, 1968); and Tamotsu Shibutani, *Society and Personality* (Englewood Cliffs, N.J.: Prentice-Hall, 1961). Social-psychological works with a psychological orientation are Edward E. Jones and Harold B. Gerard, *Foundations of Social Psychology* (New York: John Wiley & Sons, 1967); and Muzafer Sherif and Carolyn W. Sherif, *Social Psychology*, 3d ed. (New York: Harper & Row, 1969). See also Stephan P. Spitzer, *The Sociology of Personality* (New York: Van Nostrand Reinhold, 1969).

scholar's assumption of the eclecticism necessary at the time he does his work. So far as sociology is concerned, several theoretical perspectives are discernible, which perhaps makes for greater ambiguity in defining this area than the other three that I presented. However, I think it can safely be said that sociologically oriented social psychologists view their field as dealing with the effects of group experience on the origin and growth of, and changes in, the particular system of action that could be called the "personality."

Unlike other areas of sociological inquiry, social psychology focuses its attention avowedly on the individual. The principal questions to be asked are: How is the individual inducted into an ongoing social structure and, more important, how do the demands, values, and point of view of that society become part of the individual? How does he learn consistent behavior? How is he led to exercise upon himself the controls previously exercised by others? How, in short, does the individual develop a sense of himself as unique and simultaneously linked with others in a common human enterprise? As might be expected from previous discussion, the social psychologists who come from a background in sociology stress the importance of a symbolic framework of behavior, arguing that it is through the individual's manipulation of a repertoire of symbols that he and society are tied together. Attitudes, judgments, evaluations, responses to group pressure, all are ultimately symbolic constructs which, when interpreted by the individual, eventuate in some sort of action. These social psychologists therefore contend that human behavior is not merely sets of responses to sets of stimuli; the human is not a variety of pumping mechanism that "receives" at one end and "discharges" at the other. The symbol permits reflection about action before the person acts. Humans do not simply *respond;* they *initiate* behavior. The social psychologist wishes to explore how the symbolic linkage of the single human being with the containing society influences both individual and group activity.

This orientation has been less susceptible to rigorous and controlled research because, on the whole, it has been difficult to define precisely the concepts to be used and, hence, the procedures by which to test them. The studies that have emerged have been largely descriptive and limited to a few cases or, at best, rather small samples. Yet it is precisely here, I submit, that sociologists confront the human drama in all its richness. Who could not be entranced by that subtle alchemy by which people come to share a common life as they shed the dependence of childhood for the relative independence of the adult? Who could not be fascinated by the flowering of the human personality, or appalled by that deprivation which may stifle its growth, perhaps even as it begins? In no other area of the discipline of sociology does one sense so strongly the combination of art and science, regardless of the school of social-psychological thought that is applied.

Collective behavior[29] defines both what I described earlier as pluralistic, unorganized behavior and activity that marks the transition from unorganized to organized behavior and, perhaps eventually, persistent social order. Behavior that is common or collective but unorganized lacks the consensus by which an aggregation can act consistently over time. If a number of people are to survive as a group, standards of expectations and obligations must be developed and responsibilities assigned. The larger the number of people who may be involved, the more difficult this becomes. Ultimately, this transformation involves a shift from behavior based on emotional contagion rooted in the passions of the moment to behavior based on a shared symbolic framework.

Sociologists interested in collective behavior study such phenomena as crowds and mobs, panics and riots, fads and crazes, fashions, rumor and propaganda, the formation of publics, public opinion, and social movements. Students of collective behavior have contributed significantly to an understanding of the riots in Watts, Newark, and Detroit, of

[29] See n. 9, above.

disaster or its threat, of the fear engendered by rumors and predictions of everything from "mad monsters" roaming the streets of an Illinois city to the impending end of the world, and of the emergence of such disparate groups as Christians and the Communist Party.

The *sociology of small groups*,[30] which stems in part from the work of Simmel, seeks to use groups of two to ten individuals as miniature laboratories in which to test propositions that have emerged in the study of larger associations or assumptions that relate directly to the impact of group membership on individual behavior. The small group constitutes another area in which the interests of psychologists and sociologists converge, so that practitioners in both fields appear to share a common orientation. Problem-solving processes, flow of communication, leadership, friendship choice, group pressure toward conformity, the development of group rapport, and group instability are among those matters that have been studied.

You may now have some idea of the range and variety of sociologists' interests. What can we say about the sociologists themselves?

If a sociologist is defined as a person who meets the criteria for full membership in the American Sociological Association specified in its Constitution—one who holds a Ph.D. in sociology or a closely related field, or has three years of graduate study in sociology or a closely related field, or has substantial professional competence in and commitment to sociology, as determined by the Association—there were in May, 1973, approximately six thousand such individuals, about 40 per cent of the total membership of the Association, distributed among some seventy countries. According to the

[30] See A. Paul Hare, Edgar F. Borgatta, and Robert F. Bales, eds., *Small Groups: Studies in Social Interaction*, rev. ed. (New York: Alfred A. Knopf, 1967).

latest (1968) "National Register of Scientific and Technical Personnel" compiled by the National Science Foundation, a U.S. government agency, of the 297,942 scientists who responded to the Foundation's questionnaire, 6,638, or 2 per cent, identified themselves as sociologists. Of these 3,396 (51 per cent) held the doctorate, 2,507 (38 per cent) had the master's degree, and the rest had the bachelor's degree.[31] Seventy-three per cent (4,827) of the 6,638 were employed in educational institutions. The median (a point that separates a set of quantitative values into two equal halves) salary paid to full-time employed civilian sociologists was $13,500 for those whose highest degree was the Ph.D., $9,300 for those whose highest degree was the master's, and $9,000 for those who had attained only the baccalaureate.[32] It should be remembered that these data were published in 1968; inflation in the years since then would probably add several thousand dollars to each category, but it is probably safe to say that the relative standings have remained the same. A comparison of Ph.D. median salaries of sociologists and those in other fields showed sociology to be behind the physical and biological sciences, psychology, and economics but ahead of political science, anthropology, and linguistics. Twenty-two per cent of the 6,638 sociologists in the register were women; 30 per cent of these had the Ph.D., and 62 per cent were employed in educational institutions. The median annual salary paid full-time employed women sociologists with the doctorate was $12,000, or $1,500 below that of their male counterparts.[33]

Return now to the 4,827 sociologists in the register who are employed in educational institutions. They were asked to

[31] National Science Foundation, *American Science Manpower, 1968: A Report of the National Register of Scientific and Technical Personnel* (Washington, D.C.: Government Printing Office, 1969), Appendix Table A-3, p. 52.

[32] *Ibid.*, p. 38.

[33] *Ibid.*, p. 43.

TABLE I. PRIMARY WORK ACTIVITY OF SOCIOLOGISTS
EMPLOYED IN EDUCATIONAL INSTITUTIONS

Research and development	1,003
Management or administration	455
Teaching	3,073
Consulting	12
Exploration, forecasting, reporting	27
Other	126
No report	131
Total	4,827

SOURCE: National Science Foundation, *American Science Manpower, 1968: A Report of the National Register of Scientific and Technical Personnel* (Washington, D.C.: U.S. Government Printing Office, 1969), Appendix Table A-9A, p. 72.

indicate their "primary work activity," the job on which they spent the greatest amount of their work time. Let me inflict Table I upon you in order to indicate what these sociologists regarded as their major work activity. It will show that not all sociologists employed in colleges and universities teach, though most (63 per cent) do. Sociologists will be found not only in traditional sociology departments but also in medical and divinity schools, in urban-planning and environmental-studies units, as dormitory directors and counselors, but also as deans and campus presidents.

Sociologists also work in private industry, for units of government at all levels, for nonprofit organizations, and as independent consultants or investigators. And, of course, there are many other fields that can utilize sociological training: social work, personnel, police science, law, theology, counseling, management, and marketing, to name a few. Certainly the person with at least undergraduate training in sociology can use this training in ways limited only by the state of the economy and, perhaps, by his own ability to sell himself and his ingenuity in developing likely "markets" for his skills.

Nevertheless, it must be noted that sociology leads the sci-

TABLE II. SCIENTISTS NOT EMPLOYED, BY FIELD

Field	Number in Field	Number Not Employed	Per Cent Not Employed
Sociology	6,638	533	8.0
Linguistics	1,541	110	7.1
Chemistry	93,788	6,180	6.6
Political science	5,176	213	4.1
Anthropology	1,219	44	3.6
Physics	32,491	1,132	3.5
Mathematics	24,477	786	3.2
Psychology	23,077	744	3.1
Economics	11,510	315	2.7
Biological science	46,183	1,268	2.7
All fields*	297,942	12,707	4.3

* As listed in this table.

SOURCE: National Science Foundation, *Science Manpower*, Appendix Table A-4, pp. 53–55, as adapted by author.

entific and technical fields listed in the 1968 register in level of unemployment (see Table II). Whether this is due to the number of women who are temporarily absent from the field as wives or mothers is not clear from the data, particularly when fields are compared. A more intriguing, although admittedly more fanciful, explanation may be that, as historically sociology attracted people who were concerned about change, about righting the wrongs and injustices they saw about them, individuals currently attracted to and trained in the field may view nonwork (and, by implication, "nonestablishment") alternatives as more viable avenues for inducing change. Perhaps the sociologist is more willing to drop out. In 1968, too, political unrest over civil rights, "crime in the streets," and American involvement in Southeast Asia became increasingly turbulent as the process of electing a President unfolded. It may very well be that the political sensitivity of sociologists, especially the younger ones, was such that they saw in working for a candidate a much more meaningful exercise in the application of sociological insights than working for an employer. And if we look at unemployment by age group, we find that, of the 533 sociologists listed as not employed, 201 were in the 25–29 age range. However, those data suggest still another explanation perhaps a trifle closer to reality. The National Science Foundation included students among those not employed. Those who are working toward advanced degrees, especially the Ph.D., may be employed part-time as teaching or research assistants but would not be included among the ranks of the working. Because sociology is so popular today, the number of sociology students may make for a large proportion (40 per cent if we consider only those aged 25–29, 50 per cent if we add the "under 24" group) of the unemployed. Further, because work toward the doctorate is long, often requiring nine or ten years beyond the bachelor's degree, and difficult, even part-time employment must sometimes be sacrificed to the research—often out in the field—and writing necessary to secure the Ph.D. It may be that the press toward the degree proves a greater incentive than immediate full-time employment. But, regardless of the reason, the fact remains that, despite the popularity of sociology or perhaps because of it, 8 per cent of the sociologists responding to the National Science Foundation in 1968 were unemployed according to the criteria used. Moreover, there is no reason to suppose that a less healthy economy, retrenchment in governmental and academic staffs, and larger numbers of better-prepared individuals competing for available jobs have alleviated the situation since 1968.

In 1967, Norval D. Glenn and David Weiner studied 429 of those members of the American Sociological Association who had the doctorate.[34] Although all but two (included by accident) of the people studied were males, we can get at least some insight into the social characteristics of sociolo-

[34] Norval D. Glenn and David Weiner, "Some Trends in the Social Origins of American Sociologists," American Sociologist 4 (November, 1969): 291–302.

gists and how their backgrounds have changed over the years. The researchers found that, although sociology has traditionally attracted those from the Midwest and from rural areas, there have been marked declines in the proportions of Ph.D.s from these areas and an increase in the proportions from the Northeast and West. There has also been an increase in the proportion of sociologists who are Jewish and in the proportion of blacks. There has been some decline in the proportion of sociologists who come from families headed by a clergyman, but the data suggest that there has been no change over the years in the large proportion of sociologists who themselves have had ministerial training. At the same time, however, it appears that those who have become so committed to sociology as to work for the highest academic degree possible in the field have rejected religious affiliation or identification, and they appear to have done so as adolescents. Thus, contrary to what might be assumed, sociology does not "contaminate" the faith of its practitioners; rather, it appears to recruit those who were already religiously disaffected.

The sociologists who were studied also appear to have rejected the more conservative political orientations of their fathers by the time they entered adulthood. Nor have they tended to become less liberal with age. The authors observe that selective recruitment and "influences within the discipline apparently sustain liberalism."[35]

What may be most surprising is the finding that fewer than half of the respondents had an undergraduate major in sociology, although about 65 per cent majored in either sociology, psychology, or "other social sciences." Few sociologists in the sample switched to sociology from either the physical or the biological sciences. For many (although this is not developed in the investigation I am reporting) sociology was apparently a second- or third-choice occupational

[35] *Ibid.*, p. 300.

possibility when the going became difficult in chemistry or "pre-med" or mathematics; sociology seems to deal with exciting subjects, and it gives the impression of being easy, or "mickey-mouse," requiring (so it seems) little more than common sense. That sociology is not this at all is, I hope, by now obvious. Nevertheless, the view persists.

This, then, is what sociology and sociologists appear to be like in the eighth decade of the twentieth century. However, a recital of fields of interest and a display of findings about the sociologists who work in these fields cannot fully illuminate either the discipline or those who have committed themselves to it. I find being a sociologist an eminently worthwhile and rewarding venture—one might even say *adventure*—and I commend the discipline to you.

APPENDIX TO CHAPTER 3

The thirty-five subfields listed in the American Sociological Association's 1970 membership directory are as follows:

1. applied sociology
2. collective behavior
3. community
4. comparative sociology
5. crime and delinquency
6. cultural sociology
7. demography
8. deviant behavior
9. education
10. formal and complex organizations
11. human ecology
12. industrial sociology
13. law and society
14. leisure, sports, recreation, and the arts
15. marriage and the family
16. mathematical sociology
17. medical sociology
18. methodology and statistics
19. military sociology
20. occupations and professions
21. political sociology
22. race and ethnic relations
23. religion
24. rural sociology
25. small groups
26. social change
27. social control
28. social organization
29. social psychology
30. stratification and mobility
31. sociology of knowledge and science
32. theory
33. urban sociology
34. mass communications
35. economy and society

My selection of subfields for inclusion in the text and their assignment to one or another of the four major areas are arbitrary.

To satisfy your curiosity about those subfields on the ASA list that have not been discussed in the text, let me mention each of them briefly here.

Community, a field within the area of population and ecology, deals with the structure and organization of interacting persons and institutions within a particular geographic area, together with the particular attitudes, values, and perceptions that may develop out of this common residence. One of the classic papers on the subject is Simmel's "The Metropolis and Mental Life" (Wolff, ed. and trans., *Sociology of Georg Simmel* [n. 17 for Chapter 1], pp. 409–24). See also Amos H. Hawley, *Urbanization: A Study in Human Ecology* (New York: Ronald Press, 1971); Park, Burgess, and McKenzie, *The City* (n. 27 above); Arthur J. Vidich and Joseph Bensman, *Small Town in Mass Society* (Garden City, N.Y.: Doubleday Anchor Books, 1960): and Jerry D. Rose, *Introduction to Sociology* (Chicago: Rand McNally, 1971), pp. 405–17. Anthropological study is also revelant; see another "classic," by the late Robert Redfield, *The Little Community: Viewpoints for the Study of a Human Whole* (Chicago: University of Chicago Press, 1955).

Crime and delinquency, a field within the area of social organization and institutions, concerns activities that violate legal norms. Some acts have been labeled "white-collar crimes" because they are often engaged in by "respectable" people. These crimes may violate the spirit rather than the letter of the law: e.g., using the company telephone for personal calls or the company postage meter for personal mail; the executive who carries his mother-in-law on the payroll of his firm; padding expense-account vouchers. The term *delinquency* is usually applied to the illegal activities of youth. See, for example, Walter C. Reckless, *The Crime Problem*, 3d ed. (New York: Appleton-Century-Crofts, 1961); Albert K. Cohen, *Delinquent Boys: The Culture of the Gang* (Glencoe, Ill.: Free Press, 1955); and Mary Owen Cameron, *The Booster and the Snitch: Department Store Shoplifting* (New York: Free Press, 1964).

Cultural sociology, a subfield within social organization and institutions, deals with the impact of culture on human association. See Joyce O. Hertzler, *A Sociology of Language* (New York: Random House, 1965); and Mirra Komarovsky, "Cultural Contradictions and Sex Roles," *American Journal of Sociology* 52 (November, 1946): 184–89.

Deviant behavior studies all behavior (including crime and delinquency) that in one way or another is viewed as intolerable by the larger society. Obviously, what is regarded as deviant depends on both the historical period and the group that labels the offender or is itself labeled. Prostitution, compulsive gambling or drinking, and racial discrimination come to mind as examples of deviant behavior, but excessive smoking or being old or unemployable might also be regarded today as somehow unforgivable. See Howard S. Becker, *Outsiders: Studies in the Sociology of Deviance* (New York: Free Press, 1963); and Marshall B. Clinard, *Sociology of Deviant Behavior*, 3d ed. (New York: Holt, Rinehart & Winston, 1968). The area is part of social organization.

The *sociology of education* deals with the analysis of formal learning experiences as a shared enterprise. Such analysis centers about the interaction of the student, the school, and the containing social structure. Informal learning situations outside the school may also be considered. See, for example, Robert R. Bell and Holger R. Stub, *The Sociology of Education: A Sourcebook*, rev. ed. (Homewood, Ill.: Dorsey Press, 1968); Sarane S. Boocock, *An Introduction to the Sociology of Learning* (Boston: Houghton Mifflin, 1972); and Patricia Cayo Sexton, *The American School: A Sociological Analysis* (Englewood Cliffs, N.J.: Prentice-Hall, 1967). This area is also a subfield of social organization and institutions.

So is *law and society*, which investigates the relation between the structure and normative system of society and those expectations that are put on paper as laws and subject to enforcement by some agency endowed with the authority to demand compliance. See, for example, Rita James Simon, ed. *The Sociology of Law* (San Fancisco: Chandler Publishing Co., 1968).

The sociology of *leisure, sports, recreation, and the arts* is precisely that—the study by sociologists of activities presumed to deal with "play" as opposed to "work." But what about the commercial artist or the professional baseball player or the French horn player in a symphony orchestra? I regard this category as an unfortunate juxtaposition of incongruent activities. In any case, see, for example, Erwin O. Smigel, ed., *Work and Leisure: A Contemporary Social Problem* (New Haven: College and University Press, 1963); Harry Edwards, *Sociology of Sport* (Homewood, Ill.: Dorsey Press, 1973); and Joseph Bensman and Israel Gerver, "Art and the Mass Society," *Social Problems* 6 (Summer, 1958): 4–10.

Medical sociology, a subfield within social organization and institutions, concentrates on the practice of medicine as a social phenomenon. See Eliot Freidson, *Profession of Medicine* (New York: Dodd, Mead, 1970); Eliot Freidson and Judith Lorber, eds., *Medical Men and Their Work: A Sociological Reader* (Chicago: Aldine-Atherton, 1972); and David Mechanic, *Medical Sociology: A Selective View* (New York: Free Press, 1968).

Military sociology applies the techniques and perspectives of sociology to an understanding of the military establishment as a social organization and to the dynamics within that organization —what happens to individuals and groups by virtue of their inclusion within that organization—as well as the relation between the military establishment and other sectors of the larger society. See Sanford M. Dornbusch, "The Military Academy as an Assimilating Institution," *Social Forces* 33 (May, 1955): 316–21, a report on the transformation of civilian males into Coast Guard officers; Morris Janowitz, *The Professional Soldier* (Glencoe, Ill.: Free Press, 1960); and Kurt Lang, "Military Organizations," in March, ed., *Handbook of Organizations* (n. 18 above), pp. 838–78. Military sociology is a subfield of social organization and institutions.

Political sociology, within the broad area of social organization and institutions, examines the relation between the power—the ability to command—and authority, or the recognition of the legitimacy of the exercise of power, of the state in controlling social behavior and the response of a society to the controls of the state. Such matters as political involvement of a citizenry or the devices used by a government to ensure conformity are considered. The concern with the power-authority linkage was a major thread in the writings of Weber, e.g., Gerth and Mills, eds., *From Max Weber* (n. 1 for Chapter 2), pp. 46–55, 159–264. See Rose, *Introduction to Sociology*, pp. 184–212; and Scott Greer, *Governing the Metropolis* (New York: John Wiley & Sons, 1962).

The *sociology of race and ethnic relations*, again a subfield of social organization and institutions, deals with the outcome of the contacts of groups that are, or are thought to be, physically or culturally different from one another. The confrontations of black men with white men in the United States, of the Protestants with the Catholics in Northern Ireland, of Oriental Jews in Israel with those from Europe are examples of such contacts. The prejudice and hostility that result and their consequences, the process by which groups of differing social heritages may come to share a common life, the approaches such groups take to maintain and enhance their particular identities—these are all matters considered by sociologists interested in this crucial and challenging field. See, for example, S. N. Eisenstadt, *The Absorption of Immigrants* (Glencoe, Ill.: Free Press, 1955); Charles F. Marden and Gladys Meyer, eds., *Minorities in American Society*, 4th ed. (New York: D. Van Nostrand, 1972); Thomas F. Pettigrew, "Race Relations," in Robert K. Merton and Robert Nisbet, eds., *Contemporary Social Problems*, 3d ed. (New York: Harcourt Brace Jovanovich, 1971), pp. 407–65; Arnold M. Rose, "Race and Ethnic Relations," in Robert K. Merton and Robert Nisbet, eds., *Contemporary Social Problems*, 2d ed. (New York: Harcourt, Brace & World, 1966), pp. 409–78; Peter Rose, *They and We: Ethnic Relations in the United States* (New York: Random House, 1964); and Pierre L. van den Berghe, *Race and Racism: A Comparative Perspective* (New York: John Wiley & Sons, 1967).

The *sociology of religion* is also a subfield of social organization and institutions. At first glance, it might seem that religion ought to be outside the purview of the sociologist, first, because a person's beliefs ought not to be meddled with, and second because religion is eminently private, an individual preoccupation, and consequently a closed matter to the sociologist. However, it can be contended that as long as beliefs take on some group manifestations, as long as beliefs are shared—however private they may be to a particular person—religious behavior is amenable to sociological investigation. To the sociologist, it is not so much the nature of the beliefs that is important but the nature of the *believing*. The sociologist who studies religion is interested in the ways in which those who share a common perception of the "sacred" are united into a "moral community" (Durkheim, *Elementary Forms of the Religious Life* [n. 4, Chapter 2]) and thereby develop particular patterns of ideas and interaction. Such matters as the kinds and intensity of religious experience and identification, the dynamics in the development of specifically religious organizations (the difference between church, sect, and denomination, for example), and the relations between church and state and between the religious order and the economic order are of interest to the sociologist of religion. See, for example, Simmel, "Contribution to Sociology of Religion" (n. 5, Chapter 2); Weber, *Protestant Ethic and Spirit of Capitalism* (n. 6, Chapter 2); Nottingham, *Religion: A Sociological View* (n. 11, above); J. Milton Yinger, *The Scientific Study of Religion* (New York: Macmillan, 1970); and Charles Y. Glock and Rodney Stark, *Religion and Society in Tension* (Chicago: Rand McNally, 1965).

Rural sociology, part of the study of population and ecology, examines the problems and concerns that result from a shared commitment to agriculture, as well as the transformation of this commitment as a result of both encroaching urban space and technological changes in land use and processing of the products extracted from the land. See Gideon Sjoberg, "The Rural-Urban Dimension in Preindustrial, Transitional and Industrial Societies," in Faris, ed., *Handbook of Modern Sociology* (n. 2, above), pp. 127–59.

Social change is the field of sociology that attempts to take the "long view" of social life and social structure. The order in social behavior is only relative; there has always been change as one generation followed upon another, although in some periods in history change seems to have occurred much more rapidly than in others. If change is normal, shall we retreat from it or should we rather try to understand it, live with it, and learn from it, the better to prepare for the changes to come? It is usual to place social change within the framework of social organization and institutions. See, for example, Wilbert E. Moore, *Social Change* (Englewood Cliffs, N.J.: Prentice-Hall, 1963); MacIver and Page, *Society* (n. 10, Chapter 1), pp. 508–635; and Otis Dudley Duncan, ed., *William F. Ogburn on Culture and Social Change* (Chicago: University of Chicago Press, Phoenix Books, 1964). These three sources are major statements on this area.

The area of *stratification and mobility* deals with the location, distribution, and movement of individuals and aggregations of people along a ladder of statuses, which differ in the bases on which they confer power, prestige, and gratification to people in a society. We speak, for example, of the "haves" and the "have nots," the "upper crust," the "middle class," and the "disadvantaged." Whenever we define people as differing in their "life chances" or "life styles" (see Melvin M. Tumin, *Social Stratification* [Englewood Cliffs, N.J.: Prentice-Hall, 1967], p. 18), the criteria for those differences—income, education, occupation, etc.—generate the dimensions of a stratification order (or system of stratification). The sociologist wants to know the consequences for behavior of group and individual placement on such a ladder —all the way from differences in room furniture to political preference to stability of families. See also Reinhard Bendix and Seymour Martin Lipset, eds., *Class, Status and Power*, 2d ed. (New York: Free Press, 1966); E. Digby Baltzell, *The Protestant Establishment* (New York: Random House, 1964); Saul D. Feldman and Gerald W. Thielbar, eds., *Life Styles: Diversity in American Society* (Boston: Little, Brown & Co., 1972); and Edward O. Laumann, ed., *Social Stratification: Research and Theory for the 1970s* (Indianapolis, Ind.: Bobbs-Merrill, 1970).

The *sociology of mass communications*, a subfield within the broad area of social psychology, investigates the operation and effects of mass media—television, newspapers, films, radio—in society. See Otto N. Larsen, "Social Effects of Mass Communication," in Faris, ed. *Handbook of Modern Sociology* (n. 2, above), pp. 348–81; and Hadley Cantril, Hazel Gaudet, and Herta Herzog, *The Invasion from Mars* (Princeton, N.J.: Princeton University Press, 1940).

Economy and society, a subarea of organization and institutions, deals with the influence of productive, distributive, and exchange mechanisms on society. For example, competition is as much a sociological phenomenon as an economic one; if a supermarket drives away the neighborhood grocery, what happens to the network of social relations in the neighborhood? What happens to a community when the largest employer leaves for a new location? What happens to the stability of a neighborhood when the rumor of impending population shifts leads to panic selling by residents? Needless to say, it is difficult to disentangle economic behavior from other kinds of behavior, but some sociologists (as did Weber) often focus on the interplay between the economy and other sectors of the social structure. See Neil J. Smelser, "The Sociology of Economic Life," in Talcott Parsons, ed., *American Sociology: Perspectives, Problems, Methods* (New York: Basic Books, 1968), pp. 143–55.

To repeat, my selection of areas for discussion in the text, as against in this appendix, was arbitrary. I hope that after reading the text or this appendix (preferably both) you will have an idea of the varieties of sociological concern.

4

The Craft of Sociology

WE HAVE SEEN that sociology represents a particular approach to man in the world, that the approach has taken shape slowly, over centuries, and that it is not easily acquired. However, full awareness of the nature of this approach, of its ability to illuminate conduct can come only from doing sociology. Reading prepares the way for action but is obviously no substitute for action. Nevertheless, you might be able to participate vicariously in the life of the sociologist and share some of his excitement of discovery by examining three sociological analyses that are considered to be classics. They are so regarded because of the excellence of their execution and the generality of their insights. The discussion, it is hoped, will make concrete much of the material of previous pages, suggesting how the sociologist confronts human behavior and, with his special theoretical equipment, adds to our understanding of it. These three studies represent different ways of doing sociology; two of them use the "hard" data of statistics, and one is a case study. The first deals with suicide, the second with the social organization of a slum community, and the third concerns the relation between religion and the pursuit of success in metropolitan Detroit.

THE ULTIMATE COP-OUT

When we first talked about Durkheim in Chapter 2, we said that, taking his cue from Comte, Durkheim wanted to build the most positive or scientific study of social life possible. He argued that in order to do this we must focus only on the results of collective action, such as the forms of family or law or ideologies characteristic of particular groups, rather than on individual behavior. Social behavior can only be explained socially—with reference to other social facts—and never psychologically. In attempting to set forth what he regarded as the rules of sociological practice, his reliance on the primacy of collective life as against the autonomy of the individual is central, and most of his writings reflect this preoccupation. Certainly, this is the burden of his study of suicide. But our interest is less in the *why* of his investigation than in the *how*.

Durkheim's *Le Suicide* was published in 1897 (in English in 1951).[1] Then as now, most people, including other writers on the subject, tended to attribute suicide to the subjective state of the person at that moment. The individual takes his life because he is despondent or melancholy over his current predicament—financial reversals, worsening disease, unhappiness in love, or the like. Or, possibly, what Durkheim refers to as "cosmic events"—the weather, a gloomy environment, the brevity of the daylight hours in winter—might provoke in a person a mood whose end result is the ending of life.

Obviously, suicide is an intensely individual matter, but is it really so random and fortuitous as such explanations might suggest? Certainly not, Durkheim answers. And for evidence

[1] Emile Durkheim, *Suicide* (Glencoe, Ill.: Free Press, 1951).

he directs our attention to the statistics on suicides that European nations had been collecting for decades. These statistics are presented in the form of rates—so many suicides per thousand population. At the time Europe was far ahead of the United States in collecting vital statistics of all sorts, and the material on suicide constituted for Durkheim a mine of data. There are rates on suicide by sex, age, ethnic background, occupation, income, education, marital status, military service history, religion, place of residence, *ad infinitum*. If we look at these rates we will see, according to Durkheim, that suicide is by no means a haphazard occurrence but that some categories of people seem to experience a greater incidence of suicides than one would expect by chance. But why? Could some groups appear to be more genetically prone to suicide? Hardly. Could some collectivities exhibit greater insanity rates, thus producing a greater tendency to suicide (which could be conceived as a form of mental illness)? No such correlation exists.

Then we must look at the groups themselves. As sociologists we must ask if there is not perhaps a kind of social environment, a group dynamic, that might provide a climate favorable to suicide. In a truly positivist fashion, Durkheim asserts that this is in fact the case and that it is moreover the most logical approach to an understanding of the phenomenon. Let us, then, follow his logic (although not the framework in which he places it).

1. More Protestants than Catholics commit suicide. Certainly, the taking of one's life is a cardinal sin for both; it is unthinkable that Protestants could somehow be less antagonistic toward suicide than Catholics. Durkheim suggests that the answer lies less in the deposit of faith of the two groups than in the group settings which stem from Protestant and Catholic doctrine. The devout Catholic recognizes that his acceptance of the Catholic belief system binds him to a com-

munity of believers, the "mystical body of Christ," and in common all approach the Godhead through the intercessory and redemptive power of the Church. To the degree that one commits himself to Church teachings and directives, he is never alone, for he is embraced by the Church. The power of the priest to hear, absolve, and forgive provides both a ready ear and a haven in time of trouble. The more closely one is bound up in the life of (Catholic) faith, the more strength one will absorb from his fellows. Living becomes easier to bear because of the social context—knowing that, ideally, others (in addition to the heavenly Other) care as they participate in a common spiritual life.

The Protestant, however, is not so fortunate, according to Durkheim. There is no holy Mother Church to enfold him. By and large, the Protestant clergy cannot confer sacramental grace. To be a Protestant in good standing, to identify closely with Protestant Christianity, requires that the individual stand alone. He must be, *par excellence,* the *protest*ant, much as Luther had protested to the Catholic synod of bishops that was interrogating him on his Catholicity, "Here I stand [by implication, alone]—I can do naught else." The Protestant must carve out his own path to salvation. Every believer must be his own priest and find his absolution in his own way. Because the devout Protestant is religiously committed to unutterable loneliness (even though he may be at one with his God), because in time of trouble he is left to his own devices, suicide becomes a possibility, regardless of the theological stigma attached to the act.

But the Jew has the lowest suicide rate of all. Durkheim explains this by observing that, over centuries, the Jewish group has been ostracized, pursued from pillar to post, and subjected to every sort of indignity and degradation, not the least of which was death (what would Durkheim have said had he witnessed the holocaust of World War II?). Durkheim, who was himself Jewish, contended that the Jew survived because of such intense loyalty to his group that the preservation of the faith—keeping the group intact—became a joint effort and a common task. Even martyrdom was a group matter. Consequently, to commit suicide and thus threaten group stability and continuity would have been unthinkable, even if Biblical and Talmudic injunctions were not already present.

2. Married people have lower suicide rates than the unmarried—either nonmarried, widowed, or divorced. Moreover, the presence of children in the family sharply decreases the suicide rate. The explanation should be obvious. Marriage implies a community of interest which further suggests a sense of solidarity in the face of crisis. The strong sense of cohesion which preserves the family against outward threat—especially if there are relatively helpless children involved—preserves the internal solidity of the family structure. The group need not be broken because the presence of a partner at least theoretically guarantees a ready ear and a sounding board for one's troubles, a possibility (again, theoretically) unavailable to the person without a spouse.

3. Soldiers have a higher suicide rate than civilians. At first glance, it might appear that males who are physically the cream of the crop of their respective countries, who are trained to identify with their units, and who are indoctrinated with intense devotion to their nation would be immune to the pull of suicide. Perhaps, then, the answer lies in the fact that soldiers are by and large unmarried, or in the use of alcohol (or, today, narcotics) by the military, or, simply, in the objective rigors of military life. Durkheim dismisses all these factors. Alcohol, he claims, is only residually related to suicide. And suicides among the military occur with greatest frequency among officers and noncommissioned officers, both groups that tend to be married and have, we might expect, become inured to the exigencies of the soldier's lot to a far greater extent than enlisted men. Certainly, they would prob-

ably occupy better quarters, would have available to them more of the amenities of life, and would be less likely to occupy forward positions most vulnerable to enemy attack. Yet Durkheim's own statistics show that commissioned officers have higher suicide rates than noncommissioned officers, who are, in turn, more prone to suicide than draftees. And herein lies the clue he seeks.

The strong association between suicide rate and length of military service seems to suggest to Durkheim that it is not simply involvement with the group—"let's hear it from Company B"; "fifteen rahs and a yeah, team!"; "I'm from ———— and I couldn't be prouder, if you didn't hear it once I'll yell a little louder!"—that is important but the *intensity* of involvement, such that one's own accomplishments pale into insignificance in contrast to unit accomplishment. The individual becomes so strongly attached to the group that group welfare supersedes the demands of the person. The group literally (and this is perfectly in keeping with Durkheim's theoretical position) acquires a life of its own, which engulfs the person, swallows him up as if he never existed, and forces him to surrender his uniqueness and autonomy for the presumably common welfare. Hence, if one's unit fares badly —is decimated in battle, has its honor slighted, loses an interunit competition—it is as if the individual is hurt. Moreover, he shares in the collective responsibility for the sorry outcome. Suicide becomes one way of assuaging both individual and collective hurt and redeeming the unit. The relation between suicide and rank becomes eminently clear if we introduce the notion of identification intensity to explain it; the commissioned officer would be more strongly attached to his unit than would the noncom, who, in turn, would exhibit greater loyalty than the man doing his two-year hitch. There is simply a greater tendency to submerge one's self in the group.

Examples of course abound. One can think of the duels,

made famous in operettas like Friml's *Student Prince*, between German university students at the turn of the century who felt that the honor of their "corps" (fraternity) having been besmirched, death courted openly would be the only means to regain individual and group respect. Or consider the code of the Samurai warrior in feudal Japan. The Samurai was an itinerant soldier who could literally be rented for a particular mission. His philosophy was embodied in Bushido, "the way of the warrior"; its major principles included the primacy of duty before self and the assumption of death before dishonor. If such a warrior were to fail in his obligations to his lordly employer, he would be obliged to disembowel himself ceremonially as a sign of personal and social failure. The Japanese *kamikaze* (suicide) pilot of World War II, who, out of loyalty to and identification with the Emperor, dived his fighter plane into the deck of an Allied warship and of course died, was simply a more recent version of Bushido. Death, the ultimate abasement of self, offers the crowning proof of group commitment. Finally, from India comes the case of *suttee:* A husband dies and his wife, having no further reason to live, throws herself onto the funeral pyre.

4. It would surprise no one to learn that the suicide rate increases in time of financial difficulty. Durkheim's study of his statistics points up a much more surprising observation: there is a marked upswing of suicides at a time of economic revival as people are thrust with terrifying suddenness into a world of brand-new possibilities. Newfound wealth brings in its wake what I call the Cracker-Jack phenomenon: "the more you eat, the more you want." When everything appears to be attainable, there is no end to what one wants, but neither is there satisfaction. The gap between means and ends never closes, and the individual is left in the anomalous position of not knowing how to cope with success. Old norms seem inappropriate, and the vocabulary by which the new

situation might be defined and interpreted simply does not exist. Because there are no social benchmarks to order behavior, the individual, plunged as he is into sudden normative disarray, is thrown on his own devices, which prove unequal to survival in a society in upheaval. For Durkheim, the individual shorn of group ties and group demands is meaningless. Death becomes, perhaps, the only rational outcome to an utterly irrational set of circumstances.

5. We have already encountered Durkheim's fascination with divorce and the marital state. Solidity of the marriage bond, we have discovered, makes for a far lower suicide rate among married people than among bachelors, the widowed, or the divorced. But, among the widowed and divorced, is it simply dismemberment of the group and, hence, destruction of old ties and loyalties that are responsible for heightened rates? Durkheim now argues from the perspective of the person left alone. The path of loneliness is indeed a difficult one to travel. To be sure, others have passed this way before, but they have left few if any clues as to how one ought to proceed. Obviously, we have today such groups as Parents Without Partners; in the last century, all that could be held out to the widowed was sympathy, to the divorced scorn or ridicule, particularly if the person involved were a female. Without shared norms that govern action, building a life is a fruitless undertaking, for then one is like the builder of a home who works without plans. The result is a chaos of confusing demands which may be all but surmountable for far too many. Death, at least, is final; there is no confusion in the solitude, the eternal loneliness, of the grave.

We have just looked at five suicide-rate differentials and the explanations Durkheim advanced for each of them: the religious variable, the marriage variable, the military service variable, the economic cycle as a variable, and the severance of relationships—loneliness—as a variable. What apparently fascinated Durkheim, and is still fascinating after almost a century, is the common chord that resonates through *each* of these cases, which permits a single sociological factor to account for them all (and this is what makes *Suicide* a classic). This is the factor of social solidarity or cohesion. To see why this should be the case, let us review his analyses once again.

Catholics, as a group, tend to commit fewer suicides than Protestants because of common ties that afford a refuge in crisis not available to the Protestant. From the Protestant vantage point, there is cohesion, too, but of a different sort because it stems from different values. The Protestant who wishes to be in "good standing" (here we are reinterpreting Durkheim) must paradoxically stand alone to be involved; in order to demonstrate involvement in the Protestant world view he is literally required to divest himself of group anchorages. So suicide may occur when for him there is nowhere interpersonally—and yet everywhere doctrinally—to turn for solace. Like Rousseau's political man who rebels against the will of the majority, the commitment of the Protestant forces him to be free. Jews must stay together lest the religiocultural group be destroyed.

Those who are married exhibit lower suicide rates than the unmarried precisely because of the solidarity implicit in marital interaction; life is worth preserving when it is seen as worthy by another, when common goals and values provide the stuff of a shared endeavor.

Commissioned officers in the armed services exhibit a higher suicide rate than enlisted men because of a sense of identification with their units, which makes self-sacrifice legitimate; the preservation of the integrity of the group takes precedence over the integrity of the person.

A sudden transformation of fortune, whether for good or ill, deprives the person of group-linked normative expectations of behavior. Without the cues to conduct provided by the group, the individual is unable to interpret what goes on around him in order that he might make sense of his changed circumstances. So there appears a higher suicide rate in times of precipitous economic change.

Finally, the individual who, to all intents, literally "loses" his group and the involvements that go with it and who finds himself alone—like the widowed—cannot cope with a situation utterly devoid of the anchorages provided by a cohesive group. The high suicide rate among such individuals suggests their form of "adjustment."

In every case mentioned by Durkheim, the explanatory factor for high rates of suicide among particular groups is the quality or intensity of the solidarity, the cohesion, the feeling of "groupness" that may be present. Thus, Durkheim ties together seemingly different phenomena by linking them all to a single and eminently sociological variable. His analysis therefore meets a fundamental criterion of "good" scientific explanation—that it be simple. In addition, the explanation is *sociological*. Suicide is viewed as a social phenomenon, and it can be explained only in terms of another social phenomenon (or "social fact"): the fact of the group attachments themselves. Moreover, Durkheim demonstrates his thesis with the simplest of data—tables of suicide rates—and with a minimum of statistical operations; in fact, he had to invent his own as he went along because the science of statistics was in its infancy. And last, his analysis has the quality that has been called "fruitful." This means that researchers who came after Durkheim could apply his explanation of suicides to phenomena wholly unrelated to suicide and achieve not only a greater understanding of the process at hand but predictive ability previously unavailable. Because this ability lies precisely at the heart of the scientific outlook, *Suicide* stands as a monument to the accumulation of scientific sociological knowledge both in its own right and in the many studies that followed in its conceptual path. It is to such a later, and very different, investigation that I turn now.

SLUM

Slum! The word sounds unpleasant. Its origin is unknown, but it conjures up the stench of poverty, of filth, of vice and dissolution in all their forms. One has the sense of hordes of uncouth and unlettered *others*—so different from whatever we may be—all struggling to survive and overcome those inborn defects of character responsible for their deplorable condition. Try as they might, such people can never acquire those qualities of civility and breeding that so clearly differentiate *us* from *them*. The denizens of the slum ought therefore to be avoided lest we become contaminated, or should at least be afforded the kind of splendid isolation one might offer an exotic beast—curiosities, certainly, but never quite real.

Although sociologists ought to have known better, they too succumbed to such a view of the slum. In the first several decades of this century, sociologists approached slum communities as illustrative of the pathological, the sick, in social life. They uncritically assumed that modal behavior—what "most people" do—is normal behavior, which should, over time, tend to bring all the parts of society into stable, harmonious equilibrium. Behavior that lies outside the norm and therefore limits the drive toward stability of the social structure must be by definition non-normal and, therefore, bad. It was customary to speak of "social organization" as a desirable state of affairs, while "social disorganization" was a symptom of the poor social health underlying some parts of the society. When the sociologist examined the hobo or the prostitute or the conflict of immigrant cultures with the dominant American ethos, he did so within this context. Over the years, then, the slum received a "bad press"—in sociology as elsewhere.[2]

[2] See C. Wright Mills, "The Professional Ideology of Social Pathologists," *American Journal of Sociology* 49 (September, 1942): 165–80;

Needless to say, sociology has since grown up. An equilibrium model of social life has been supplanted by others. Sociologists ideally operate as ethically neutral reporters of the human scene without evaluating the behavior they study. Conduct is neither intrinsically good nor bad, neither sick nor healthy. These adjectives are applied by the larger society. While the sociologist may work with such labels as indicative of group evaluations, he argues for the notion of deviancy—a non-normative label applied to behavior that exceeds the limits of toleration current in particular population aggregates. These limits change as values change. In 1900, for example, a woman who smoked a cigarette or who exposed her ankles to public view was looked upon as debauched, "loose." Obviously, our values have changed since 1900. Therefore, when studying values *as data* and the resulting behavior *as data* the label of deviancy is shorn of any pejorative connotations, and the sociologist is freed of evaluational demands.[3]

Gunnar Myrdal, *An American Dilemma* (New York: Harper & Bros., 1944), pp. 1035-64; and Alvin W. Gouldner, *The Coming Crisis in Western Sociology* (New York: Basic Books, 1970).

[3] This, of course, raises the thorny question of whether the sociologist ought to evaluate, whether he is obliged to make moral judgments. Here we must distinguish between the role of the sociologist as citizen and his role as man of knowledge. As a citizen, indeed as a knowledgeable and responsible human being, the sociologist must make choices and take stands. He ought to be a committed human being. This involves the determination of good and bad and right and wrong within some evaluative framework that the sociologist holds dear; probably it derives from the normative tradition of the society of which he is a part. If he has his wits about him he will base his professional scholarly life on certain value premises. He may study *x* because he feels it is not only worthwhile in itself but is also an aspect of the human condition that demands a solution. He may refuse to study *y* because it offends his moral sense. All this is as it should be. But once the sociologist begins his work and assumes the mantle of scholarly detachment, he must remain ethically neutral. He cannot let his values override his scientific attitude. And concepts without an emotional overlay, like deviancy, help him to accomplish this.

The study I want to discuss now is indicative of, and perhaps to some degree responsible for, a break with the tendency on the part of some sociologists to moralize about their work. *Street Corner Society: The Social Structure of an Italian Slum,* by William Foote Whyte, was first published in 1943; a second edition, with an extensive discussion of the research procedure, appeared in 1955.[4]

Whyte is the product of a solid and utterly respectable middle-class background. As an undergraduate at Swarthmore he majored in economics, wrote stories and plays, engaged in several efforts at social reform—including an abortive attempt to eliminate the fraternity system at his college —and saw himself as a permanent part of "the Establishment." However, as part of a class project, he visited a Philadelphia slum. Whyte came away from the experience wanting to help "these people," but with no idea of how to begin. He knew only that he wished in some way to transcend his social heritage and learn about another portion of his world, to learn fully and intimately in a manner no book or professor could teach. His opportunity came when he was elected to a fellowship at Harvard.

Election to the Society of Fellows of Harvard carried with it the stipulation that the recipient would be supported for three years of graduate study, during which he could *not* work toward the Ph.D.; whatever he undertook would be solely for his own intellectual growth. Whyte chose, after several false starts, to satisfy his curiosity about the slum. He focused on the Italian section of South Boston—an area he called "Cornerville" in his work—as the "ideal" slum, at least in terms of what he thought typified such an area. As an economist he started out interested particularly in housing, patterns of consumption, and the distribution of goods and services within Cornerville. But the longer he walked about the neighborhood, the more he tried to get to know its citi-

[4] Published by the University of Chicago Press.

zens, and the more he read, the more he realized that he was becoming less an economist and increasingly a sociologist. He began to think as a sociologist, to become concerned with "social attitudes" and the interaction between the community and the people who lived in it. He realized that while sociologists had talked about the slum and investigated aspects of it, there had never been an in-depth study of such a community. He decided that was the task for him.

Whyte was able to find a room with an Italian family. (This took some doing, for Cornerville residents were suspicious of outsiders, but it must be remembered that at the time the United States was only beginning to emerge from the ravages of the Depression of the 1930's, and additional income was always welcome.) He began to study Italian and attempted to meet people. At first he naïvely tried to "horn in" on dating couples; as a result, he was told that he *and* his science might be ousted from a community gathering place. Then he tried the Norton Street Settlement House as a possible point of entry into Cornerville. There a social worker introduced him to Doc, a member of a corner gang, who eventually became one of his principal informants. They hit it off, and the study began.

Whyte bowled and drank, dated, and took part in the political life of Cornerville. As he participated in the affairs of the slum, he observed what he saw around him, taking copious notes and organizing them in various ways as his familiarity with Cornerville grew. During the study Whyte married. The couple rented an apartment of their own in the neighborhood and new avenues of communication opened as husband—and wife—became further involved in the Cornerville ethos. And the more Whyte immersed himself in his surroundings, the more clearly he saw the importance of the group for the determination of the particular life style of Cornerville.

Whyte found the social fabric of the neighborhood to be

composed in part of formal and informal groups of late adolescents and young adults who "hung out" on street corners
in Cornerville (thus the title of his book). Such habitual association usually dated from boyhood, and while school attendance and movement within and from the Italian community might change regularity of attendance on the corner,
group membership remained relatively stable over time as allegiance to the same corner persisted among its habitués
even after marriage. Social activities away from the corner
were organized with similar regularity and centered about a
nearby bowling alley. In addition, a regular meeting place
aside from the corner was used—a cafeteria or tavern, where
the group sometimes gathered after bowling or some other
activity and before returning to the corner or going home.
Because behavior was thus rigid in proceeding along pre-
scribed lines, individual group members exhibited a marked
lack of interpersonal assurance except when the group inter-
acted together, and the group was relatively aimless as a unit
unless its acknowledged leader was present. A system of mutual obligations—who can do what for whom—existed that
served to distribute prestige among the membership. This set
of reciprocal expectations resulted from differentials in skill
in activities valued by the group, notably bowling, baseball,
and pickups. As previously implied, the leader was the focal
point of club organization. He was regarded as the most
level-headed and resourceful member of the group. The
leader usually originated action for the group or, less often,
initiated action through another, who, in turn, transmitted it
to the group as a whole.

All this might seem perfectly plausible but hardly deserv-
ing of the extended discussion Whyte provides. Nevertheless,
when he argues that these groups constituted the fabric of
Cornerville he is suggesting that they served to unify the
community—in fact, to create a sense of community. By tying
together ethnicity, political participation, and racketeering

(albeit in varying degrees, depending upon the group) as positive values, gang membership becomes an avenue of mobility through Cornerville and, on occasion, even out of it. Moreover, the community sees that it can get things done through the gang that could not be accomplished through "usual" channels of communication. In other words, the gangs continually demonstrate their "clout" to the populace and reinforce communal perceptions of them as effective agencies of change. In addition, by sanctioning rigid and regularized relations between members, the gang presents such interaction to the community as appropriate for emulation. Consequently, that interaction condoned by the group transforms Cornerville into the group writ large.

For Whyte, then, the implications of his investigation are clear. If the gangs provide an image of the society as a closely knit structure in which people are related to one another through a hierarchy of defined and recognized claims and obligations, it would hardly be fair to brand Cornerville as in any sense disorganized. Rather, Cornerville's organization simply does not mesh with the organization of larger Boston; the two are interdependent without being integrated. And it is the failure of these two structural entities to come together that constitutes the problem not only for Cornerville or, indeed, any slum community but for the integration of a nation of immigrants. How much Whyte, writing in the 1940's, foreshadowed the current discomforts of black, Spanish, and Mexican Americans as they try to come to terms with several heritages in the search for a viable identity.

Our society values mobility, says Whyte. Italians no less than other Americans wish to move up the ladder of success, however it may be measured, but they are blocked in two ways. The dominant society will not accept the Italian as an equal, nor will the Italian's own structure permit him to cut the ties that bind him to Cornerville. If the Cornerville resident is thus constrained to remain in his neighborhood, how might his life there be made more livable? Obviously, there are tangible concerns: better housing, more jobs, a greater variety of consumer goods at prices Cornerville people can pay. But what most concerned the Cornerville resident at the time of Whyte's study—and the core of concern among minority groups today—was what might be called respect, a sense of worth in the eye of the beholder. The Italian of South Boston wanted to feel that his contributions to American life were as valued as those of the Greek or Pole. He wished to govern himself within the social organization he had created; he did not wish the terms of his existence to be set by outsiders. His forebears had produced a Leonardo, a Michelangelo, a Verdi; he needed no one to question his motives or his life style at this stage of his history. Doc, a major gang leader and Whyte's principal informant, put it to the author of *Street Corner Society* this way (and Whyte concludes the book with this quotation):

"You don't know how it feels to grow up in a district like this. You go to the first grade—Miss O'Rourke. Second grade—Miss Casey. Third grade—Miss Chalmers. . . . At the fire station it is the same. None of them are Italian.

"Now you must know that the old-timers here have a great respect for schoolteachers and anybody like that. When the Italian boy sees that none of his own people have the good jobs, why should he think he is as good as the Irish or the Yankees? It makes him feel inferior. . . .

"Bill, . . . the second generation is growing up and we're beginning to sprout wings. They should take that net off and let us fly."[5]

[5] William F. Whyte, *Street Corner Society: The Social Structure of an Italian Slum* (Chicago: University of Chicago Press, 1943), p. 276.

What distinguishes *Street Corner Society* is its unabashedly sociological character. Whyte began his investigation as an economist, he ended as a sociologist. The volume reflects his growing realization that, in the final analysis, one cannot understand economic or political or religious behavior without an understanding of the interaction of social individuals, behaving economically, politically, or religiously. He was led to ask, as was Durkheim before him, how group cohesion affects behavior. But unlike Durkheim, he did not accept the solidarity of groups as given. Rather, he asked how this sense of group involvement and identity is built up and maintained over time. Then, having answered that question, he effectively demonstrated the impact of the character of the group—its form, values, goals—on the larger social structure. Cornerville is thus a representation at one structural level of the process or dynamics at another. So it turns out that, when all is said and done, Whyte is as much a student of Simmel as of Durkheim; he began with the interaction of individuals and observed how larger social configurations—like communities—become crystallizations of underlying forms or processes of interaction. Whatever Whyte may have intended, he emerges from the pages of his book every inch a sociologist.

The sociological character of the study emerges, too, in the finding that, contrary to popular opinion, however much Cornerville may be a slum, it nevertheless exhibits an identity, a uniqueness, a social organization of its own. For to the sociologist, no aggregation of individuals lacks a structure, even if it is only in the process of organization or becoming. Such a statement sounds eminently reasonable in the abstract. However, when the contention is applied to particular human aggregations, many people tend to defer to "popular opinion," which is often elevated to the level of common sense. Whenever a group is defined as in any sense "different" it is taken as different *in toto*. And what this really implies is that "they" are not quite as good as "we" are. From living room to life style, "we" are pure, "they" are not. While such a perspective may permit acceptance of our own situation and permit us to come to terms with our fate, for there are always "others" who are more unfortunate, more put upon than "we," this perspective can keep us from observing flesh-and-blood people, who, in their situation, are as fearful of us as we are of them.

So one could say that sociology is subversive. Its orientation does violence to our nice, neat perspectives; it suggests that "common sense" may be common but hardly sensible. Sociology implicitly argues—and the message comes out clearly in *Street Corner Society*—that all human beings exhibit similar sociocultural forms of interaction, and that the necessity or even the inevitability of difference should not obscure the common road we all travel toward the common destiny of death. When William Whyte suggests that, like it or not, these different and exotic and somehow suspicious Italians of Cornerville have structured their community in terms of the same values that appear to animate all Americans, his analysis is simply a further illustration of the sociologist's concern for the unvarnished depiction of social reality, to "tell it like it is," and in so doing lay to rest those cherished myths that, in the shadow of the atomic cloud, have no survival value whatever.

Finally, Whyte's study is a gem of the sociological craft because it is, throughout, concerned with people—understanding them and working with them and for them in the hope that what one other human being, who also happens to be a sociologist, may accomplish will ultimately enrich and ennoble the lives of all. Whyte shows how, ideally, the sociologist becomes a part of the world of those he studies and *participates* as he *observes*. The more he immerses himself, the more he learns. Yet, as a scientist, the sociologist has learned how to detach himself from his subjects just enough to resist the ever present temptation to become so completely at one with them that he "goes native." One can of course be trained to such discipline. The concern, however, is not a value that can be acquired formally. In fact, I am not at all sure how one does come by it. But, again ideally, the sociologist must have it, whether he observes his subjects directly or operates indirectly through survey data. Whyte thus brings intellectual curiosity out of the classroom, out of the library, and couples it to a belief in the worth of the individual. That is the concern which comes across in the pages of *Street Corner Society* and makes the book such a readable and provocative introduction to sociology as science and to sociologists as scientists.

THE ELEVENTH COMMANDMENT: THOU SHALT SUCCEED

When Karl Marx in the middle of the last century damned religion as the opiate of the people he was simply varying the theme—albeit spectacularly—that runs throughout all his writings: the economic organization is the base on which all social life rests, including the systems of ideology and belief (i.e., religion). Some forty years later Max Weber decided to challenge the validity of the Marxian hypothesis and thereby set off a debate still unresolved.

Weber's challenge to Marx is contained in what is probably his most widely known work, *The Protestant Ethic and the Spirit of Capitalism*. His argument is that the productive and exchange mechanisms of any society can flourish only if there exists a constellation of values congenial to these mechanisms. It is rather like saying that bacteria can multiply only in an appropriate biological medium. He bases his case on an intensive examination of the theology of Calvinist Protestantism and asserts that the values of this branch of the Protestant communion—sobriety, thrift, hard work for no reason other than that diligent labor glorifies God, the accumulation of money as a sign of God's favor (which must of course be plowed back into the business)—provided a climate of belief favorable to the emergence of capitalism as a way of economic life.[6] He demonstrates to his own satisfaction that, where Protestantism flourished, so did capitalist enterprise; the United States becomes a first-class illustration of his contention.

While sociology has largely accepted Weber's argument, the debate nevertheless continues, and reports of attempts to validate the argument regularly appear in the periodicals of the profession. I want to consider one of them, with less interest in the ability of the piece either to support or refute Weber than as an example of elegant contemporary quantitative sociological research. The paper, by Albert J. Mayer and Harry Sharp, is entitled "Religious Preference and Worldly Success" and appeared in the *American Sociological Review* in April, 1962 (pp. 218–27).

The authors wonder about the applicability of the tenets of the Protestant Ethic to the population of a large American city, in this case Detroit, Michigan, and particularly as differing religious experiences (represented by denominational labels) may be related to variations in secular achievement. Mayer and Sharp assume, on the basis of Weber's work, that Roman Catholic belief orients adherents toward an other-worldly existence, so that achievement in the market place and the acquisition of goods emblematic of success take on relatively little importance in this world; Protestants, on the other hand, could be expected to be oriented toward the attainment of those things that bespeak economic success, prestige, and movement up the social ladder and, therefore, salvation in the here-and-now. Therefore, it might be pre-

[6] We have only scratched the surface of Weber's analysis. To do more would take us far afield from the direction I would like to travel. Needless to say, *The Protestant Ethic* is itself a classic of sociological literature and is worth confronting on its own terms.

dicted that Protestants would outstrip Roman Catholics in the drive toward success in the world. Further, variations might be expected within Protestantism, which is hardly a homogeneous faith in contemporary America, in adherence to the Protestant Ethic and consequently in economic achievement. Put very generally, then, the authors hypothesize that differing religious preferences are associated with differing degrees of economic success.

Mayer and Sharp then attempt to place Jews and adherents of Eastern Orthodoxy in the Weberian perspective. Noting, as one might expect, that these groups do not fit the model, the authors argue that, as Jews played a supporting role in the emergence of capitalism (at least in terms of the documentation they offer), it could be hypothesized that Jews would lie closer to Protestants on a scale of economic achievement than they would to Roman Catholics. The writers chose not to suggest an explanation for Eastern Orthodox achievement.

Having laid the conceptual groundwork for their study, Mayer and Sharp turn to the study itself. If, they say, life in the modern city can be viewed as a kind of marathon in which families compete for material reward and the status and success that result from a race well run, then the hypothesis of the study would suggest that different religious groups will fare more or less well in the contest; some will "win," some will "place," still others will "show," and there will be denominations that will be "also rans" in the competition for the things that, in our society, bespeak success. But —and it is an important "but"—religious affiliation is a socioeconomic variable that does not exist in the life of the individual in isolation from other socio-economic attributes. A person who is, let us say, a member of the Lutheran Church of America or of the Disciples of Christ or of the Southern Baptist Convention is *also*, perhaps, a city dweller, a worker in a particular job, native-born with a high school education, married for umpteen years, and whatever other characteristics one might wish to include. One must therefore ask if, as the hypothesis of the investigation suggests, religious affiliation and the values that stem from it operate *directly* to produce varying degrees of economic well-being or whether other factors that may accompany a particular religious preference are instrumental in promoting the success of the particular religious group. To put it in another way (almost, but not quite, statistically), how much does religion itself account for the achievement of a religious group, as against other, nonreligious factors that may be operating at the same time? The investigator is therefore constrained to design a study that gets at such variations in causation. Mayer and Sharp claim they have done so by looking at the relation between religious preference, achievement variables (what members of the group have actually accomplished), and ascribed variables (attributes attached to group members without any action on their part, such as age, sex, ethnic background and the like). At the same time they say they recognize that not all religious denominations may be favored equally with the background factors that might be conducive to economic success in the city. Consequently, they devised a system of "handicapping" to take account of this by ensuring statistically that all groups have an equal advantage at the start of the race. Thus, the ascribed variables would not unfairly exaggerate group differences, and the relation of religion to the achievement variables could be seen more clearly. Hence the hypothesis would be easier to test because it would be more "visible."

Now to the data themselves. The University of Michigan since 1952 has been conducting a study of the Detroit metropolitan community. In addition to eliciting valuable information of all kinds about the dynamics of a complex urban community, the Detroit Area Survey has served as a superb training ground for graduate students in sociology at that university. Mayer and Sharp used data collected between 1954 and 1959, treating all of it as a single unit, from every adult who lived at specific, randomly chosen addresses in metropolitan Detroit. These adults were then classified by religious affiliation in terms of their answers to the following questions:

Do you have a religious preference?

If yes, are you Protestant, Catholic, Jewish, or something else?

If Protestant, what specific denomination?

For analytical purposes the authors then grouped the sample into twelve denominational categories:

a. Catholic
b. Jewish
c. Eastern Orthodox
d. Episcopalian
e. Lutheran
f. Calvinist[7]
g. Methodist
h. Baptist
i. Small neo-fundamentalist Protestant sects[8]
j. Nondenominational Protestant
k. Semi-Christian churches[9]
l. No religious preference

(It ought to be noted here, just for the record, that I am merely *reporting* what Mayer and Sharp did; the classification scheme is theirs. If you are unhappy with it, blame them.) The character of the sample is shown in Table III.

The researchers begin the description of their findings by analyzing the relation between differences in denominational achievement and ascribed factors—the rural-urban dimension, the foreign born–native born dimension, and the extent

[7] The authors include Presbyterians, Congregationalists, Evangelical and Reformed, and Dutch Reformed churches.

[8] Exemplified by the Jehovah's Witnesses and Pentecostal churches.

[9] The authors regard this category as including groups that might not be classified elsewhere, such as the Church of Jesus Christ Latter Day Saints (Mormons), Church of Christ, Scientist, spiritualist churches, and the like.

TABLE III. DISTRIBUTION OF MAYER-SHARP SAMPLE BY
RELIGIOUS AFFILIATION AND RACE

	Number of Cases
White	
Catholic	3,307
Protestant	
Episcopalian	289
Lutheran	778
Calvinist	723
Methodist	750
Baptist	727
Small Sects	232
No denomination	194
Semi-Christian	96
Total White Protestant	3,789
Jewish	234
Eastern Orthodox	169
No Preference	239
Total White	7,738
Black	
Catholic	75
Methodist	316
Baptist	938
Other	164
Total Black	1,493
Total Sample	9,231

SOURCE: Adapted from Mayer and Sharp, "Religious Preference and Worldly Success," *American Sociological Review* 27 (April, 1962): Table 1, p. 221.

of experience in the Detroit metropolitan area. It was assumed that, at one extreme, they might find a religious group all of whose members were born in the United States of native-born fathers, who had no rural background and had spent their entire adult lives in the Detroit ambit; at the other pole of this hypothetical continuum one might find a group all of whose members were of foreign birth and had a rural background and little or no experience in the urban setting. Would it not seem reasonable, then, to assume that the first group described would have a considerable advantage over its polar opposite in the achievement of success in the urban milieu, since they would have had maximal exposure to it and its values? In other words, the greater the familiarity with the environment, the greater the ascribed advantage. "Well, then," they said, "let us plot the position of the various religious denominations on such a continuum." And what they find looks something like Figure 1 (after "handicapping" and necessary statistical manipulation to make all the findings comparable):

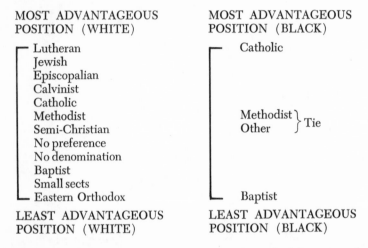

Figure 1. Continuum illustrating impact of ascribed factors on denominational achievement.

In turning to the performance of their religious denominations, Mayer and Sharp used five indicators of achievement: percentage of each group earning $2,000 or more above the median Detroit income indicated by continuing Detroit Area Study findings; percentage of each group who are self-employed; percentage who are professionals, managers, proprietors, or officials (a standard U.S. Census category understood as indicating high-prestige occupational performance); median school years completed by the members of each denomination; and percentage of persons in each religious grouping who are members of three or more formal organizations. After statistical manipulation to make the findings on these five variables comparable, the authors generated a continuum similar to that of Figure 1, but this time showing the ranking of the religious groups solely in terms of achievement:

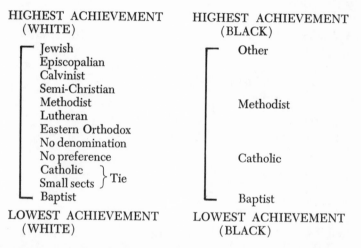

HIGHEST ACHIEVEMENT (WHITE)

- Jewish
- Episcopalian
- Calvinist
- Semi-Christian
- Methodist
- Lutheran
- Eastern Orthodox
- No denomination
- No preference
- Catholic ⎫ Tie
- Small sects ⎭
- Baptist

LOWEST ACHIEVEMENT (WHITE)

HIGHEST ACHIEVEMENT (BLACK)

- Other
- Methodist
- Catholic
- Baptist

LOWEST ACHIEVEMENT (BLACK)

Figure 2. Continuum illustrating denominational performance on achievement variables.

We now know how the denominations rank on ascribed and achieved variables. But the real question of the study still remains: is achievement a resultant solely of denominational affiliation, or does it result from certain ascribed factors that seem to accompany religious group membership? If we could somehow "subtract" the "ascribed ranking" from the "achieved ranking," the relation between religion and achievement would stand out in greater relief, uncomplicated by nonreligious attributes. And this is exactly what the authors did. (Unfortunately, given the importance of "race" in the determination of achievement potential in the United States, the authors felt that this particular accident of birth—skin color—could not be ignored; hence, the separate listings for "black" and "white" respondents.) Mayer and Sharp sub-

tracted the ascription handicap from a weighted achievement score (to make the data comparable), removed the
ascribed factors as a kind of contaminant, and came up with
a "pure" indicator of the relationship in which they were interested, so that the final ranking of the religious groups
looks as follows:

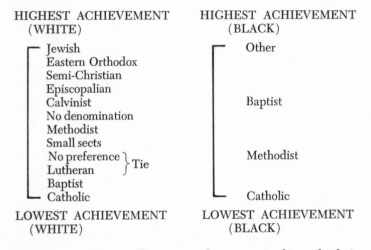

Figure 3. Continuum illustrating achievement ranking of religious
groups, taking ascription handicap into consideration.

It would appear as if Jewish, Eastern Orthodox, and "semi-
Christian" group members have achieved most, followed by
the Protestants (especially white Episcopalians and Calvin-
ists), with Catholics achieving the least economic success. In
other words, certain groups, like the Jews and the Eastern
Orthodox, have achieved worldly success *despite* extreme
handicaps such as foreign birth or non-Detroit background;
the achievement of other denominations varies little even if
one considers the role of ascribed status in the evaluation.

Mayer and Sharp interpret their findings as only partially
supporting the notion of the Protestant Ethic. There seems to
be no question that, just as Weber proposed, religious prefer-

ence is related to behavior of adherents that contributes to their economic well-being, quite apart from other associated factors. Thus, most Protestant denominations exceeded Catholicism in economic status and, among themselves, were ranked in a manner that lends further credence to Weber. Nevertheless, for other groupings, the predictability did not hold, and Mayer and Sharp present a more general cultural explanation. They suggest that the high rankings of Jews and Eastern Orthodox are due less to religious doctrine *per se* than to their sociocultural history, which, especially in the United States, led them to occupy certain occupational statuses, such as trading or shopkeeping, which fostered a success orientation. Thus, the authors argue, time may introduce factors that will alter whatever linkage there may originally have been between religion and achievement.

This, then, is what Albert J. Mayer and Harry Sharp have to say about the relation between religious preference and worldly success. I have used their article as an example of the way sociologists today use statistical data and procedures in their work. Of course, Durkheim also used statistics. But sixty years separate their undertakings, and in that time our knowledge of statistics has developed to such an extent that sociologists are now able to manipulate their data in a far more sophisticated fashion. They can use data to tell them far more about what they are studying than Durkheim could, because current techniques permit them to "get inside" their data more thoroughly than was the case in the 1890's. Moreover, the contemporary sociologist has at his disposal a variety of survey techniques that permit him to *construct* bodies of data for the specific purpose at hand. He develops a questionnaire or interview schedule that will give him the kind of information he needs to solve his problem, rather than being required, as Durkheim was, to work with material (suicide rates) already on hand. While it is true that many sociologists even today utilize existing bodies of material—vital statistics,

historical records, descriptive accounts of social organizations in process—it is equally true that large numbers of
sociologists work with statistics in the hope that mathematical exactitude can lead to scientific precision in the understanding of human affairs, the goal of all sociologists. The
article by Mayer and Sharp is an elegant example of how
such building can take place.

The authors took a qualitative theoretical orientation,
Weber's proposal of the Protestant Ethic, and presented it in
the form of a hypothesis, which they proposed to test empirically. They implied that differing degrees of "Protestantism" will eventuate in differing achievement levels. But religion is one of several socio-economic variables that adhere
to an individual. How might the religious factor be seen
more clearly? The researchers answered by rethinking, or
reconceptualizing, the religion-achievement relation to take
account of several status dimensions in which a person operates, of which religion is but one. They emerged, as we
have seen, with the "ascribed-achieved" dimension. Since
they had survey data that were eminently suitable for interpretation in terms of this dimension, the authors proceeded
to test Weber's hypothesis in this new way, and they used a
number of statistical processes, like weighting, to do it. When
they completed their investigation, they not only had a further confirmation of what Weber was trying to say, but had
learned more about the struggle to succeed in twentieth-
century America, and, incidentally, acquired additional sociological knowledge nicely and neatly.

THE END OF THE MATTER

Durkheim, W. F. Whyte, Mayer and Sharp—I believe these
three pieces of research represent sociology at its best. Matters
are examined that have implications for the lives of human beings as they attempt to function in a world that, by

and large, is not theirs to make. They represent, further, attempts to get at key sociological questions, quite apart from their human impact. The link between the individual and his groups, between ideology and performance; the relation between social cohesion and social structure—these are fundamental issues to which sociologists of every generation have addressed themselves. Obviously, these three studies provide new insights, and they are brilliantly presented by their authors. However, what is even more important—and what is the hallmark of eminent scholarship—is that they raise more questions than they answer. They lead in new research directions. They stimulate and excite others to go beyond them. Thus science grows and with it grows the potentiality for the enrichment of all of life. And, as with any learned discipline, this is what leads people to take up the sociological craft and to practice it with conviction and compassion.

5

The Age of Sociology

WHEN I TEACH I TRY TO distinguish as clearly as I can between what is known about the subject under discussion and my own views about the matter; I usually preface personal comments with the statement: "This is a purely personal prejudice." Upon hearing this, the student is prepared to take what follows with more than just a grain of salt. It could be argued that, from start to finish, this book is "a purely personal prejudice." Its organization and its content reflect my very deep conviction that sociology is worth doing because it is both intellectually satisfying and an expression of one's concern for his fellows. This is based on my assumption that knowledge *does* make a difference, that in the long run human betterment is more likely to come from reasoned and reasonable inquiry than from storming the barricades. Now, in this last chapter, I want to become even more "purely personal" by raising the question whether sociology may not already be a dying field, done to death as much by those who practice it as by those who know nothing and couldn't care less. Does sociology really have a future? Or is it destined to be consigned, like alchemy or the Platonic republic or a bygone religious dogma, to the limbo of a scholarly curiosity shop?

In asking such a question you might think that I have led you on only to let you down at the last. Sociology is demanding; it takes real work and real dedication to become a sociologist. Sociology can make a genuine contribution to an understanding of man. So go ahead. Study, sacrifice, endure all manner of trials in order to reach this eminently worthwhile goal I've been telling you about. And when you get there, what will you have? Absolutely nothing. You may argue, then, that all this verbiage you have so far read is rank dishonesty.

I won't buy that line. The possibility of a meaningful choice among alternative lines of action requires that we be aware of the consequences of our choice. We must also have some basis for the choice we make. It may be fact or considered opinion or even unconsidered emotion. But basis there must be. Hence, I regard it as imperative to acknowledge that, as useful and possibly even crucial as sociology might be, it carries in it the seeds of its own destruction. If you have a sense of this danger as well as of the wonder of sociology, you will be better able to develop a perspective in which to judge the field and, possibly, your place in it.

When Auguste Comte gave sociology a name, a program, and a place among the developing social sciences, he did not see his creation solely as a novel, albeit scientific, approach to the gathering and ordering of knowledge about human social behavior. He viewed sociology, as well, as a tool with which humanity might be released from archaic prejudices, obsolete knowledge, and outworn creeds. Humanity would be shown to be creator rather than mere consumer of ideologies. Comte took the optimistic view that revolution and riot would give way to reasoned and orderly social change once there was a science that could present knowledge and analyze social processes in such a fashion as to indicate clearly what the direction of change ought to be. Sociology was born, then, out of a desire to protest as well as to discover, and the early sociologists who followed Comte adhered to such an imagery of their calling. Men of the stamp of Simmel or Park or Weber could not see knowledge apart from action; their lives as well as their work reflected this unity.

But by 1918 Weber was writing about the "disenchantment of the world," which he saw at the core of the human condition. By the end of World War I Europe lay in waste; that war was unparalleled in its fury and in the paucity of excuses for waging it. Bombs had rained from the sky, and the world would never be the same again.

The sociologist was not immune to that "disenchantment." His hopes for a rational and therefore predictable world had been extinguished by the smoke and poison gas of French battlefields. The seemingly inexorable thread of history had been broken by the assassin's bullet that touched off that war, and the belief that rational men could dream as well as discover, that they could learn from their mistakes and presumably not make the same mistakes again, faded in the flames. The sociologist dismounted from his charger and became a "scientist."

No longer would the sociologist fight the good fight, raking up the muck alongside the best of the "yellow journalists," "telling it like it is," albeit in proper scholarly fashion and with due attention to the establishment of verified and predictable relationships. Now, operating with an orientation largely set by Weber and Durkheim, the sociologist was to observe and analyze and do all the things he did before, but dispassionately, with a studied aloofness precluding any emotional involvement in the phenomena studied. He would be ethically neutral and thereby would unearth the Truth, so long hidden behind a cloak of maudlin "concern" or empathy or just plain pity. He might get his hands dirty, but he would be safe.

Ironically, perhaps, this image of sociology as a knowledge-gatherer and nothing more took root in the same milieu that had earlier nurtured an ethic of change. This "new" image was typified in the appearance of what could be called the first real textbook of sociology (as opposed to commentaries on the social scene or on the nature of man, masquerading as sociology), *Introduction to the Science of Sociology* by Robert E. Park and Ernest W. Burgess, published in 1921 and reprinted in 1924. So influential did this book become that, for several decades, it was known as the "Green Bible" (from the color of its cover), and, when it was out of print (it was reprinted in 1969 at three times the cost of the original), copies sold on the academic "black market" for as much as fifty dollars. Both authors were on the faculty of the University of Chicago. They argued in positivist fashion that all the speculation in the world doesn't make a science. The science of sociology is here right now; there is a body of fundamental principles that can be delineated and expanded through rigorous, quantitatively oriented research. Moreover, said the authors, change itself is a fundamental social process, which can be studied and analyzed and predicted but by no means can or should be induced by the sociologist. He is not a social engineer. Sociology and social work were to go their separate ways.[1]

There were several consequences of this scientific stance—again, from my purely personal perspective.

In his search for the scholarly respectability ideally implicit in the scientific orientation, the sociologist far too often confused means and ends. If scientific inquiry is nothing more than a rigorous and controlled search for the best available answers to questions that themselves have been clearly specified within some theoretical framework, it becomes uncomfortably clear—you need only pick up at random an issue of a sociological periodical, either recent or yellowed with age—that the sociologist has concentrated on the tools and

[1] See Lee Braude, " 'Park and Burgess': An Appreciation," *American Journal of Sociology* 76 (July, 1970): 1–10.

techniques of analysis, with scant attention to the relation between the resulting evidence and the real world of flesh-and-blood humans. He has manufactured statistical procedures of monumental complexity, sophisticated questionnaires and scales and interview procedures, and a language that reads like a combination of a computer program and the instructions accompanying the federal income tax form.[2] But, by and large, the mountain labored and brought forth a mouse. The famous sociological theorist Robert K. Merton observed that sociological insight seems to consist of a collection of minor working hypotheses incidental to the conduct of research—isolated signposts on a road for which the map is yet to be created.[3] There seemed to be no way of bringing all sorts of data together at some higher level of abstraction. Moreover, the sociologist appeared to equate science with communication in a closed corporation; if only your colleagues can understand you, how bright you must really be! And if even they can't understand you, you must be all the more brilliant.[4]

Perhaps it was such a hope that led some sociologists to seek scientific legitimacy, as it were, in the other direction. It was argued that the growth of scientific knowledge results only when one has a kind of metaphysics of sociology, a grand theoretical scheme, to provide a basis for the conduct of inquiry. Such approaches, notably in the work of Talcott

[2] See Gouldner, *Coming Crisis of Western Sociology* (n. 2 for Chapter 4); the entire July, 1972, issue of *American Journal of Sociology*, dealing with "Varieties of Political Expression in Sociology" (vol. 77); Alvin W. Gouldner, " 'Varieties of Political Expression' Revisited," *American Journal of Sociology* 78 (March, 1973): 1063–93; Robert W. Friedrichs, *A Sociology of Sociology* (New York: Free Press, 1970); and Larry T. Reynolds and Janice M. Reynolds, eds., *The Sociology of Sociology* (New York: David McKay, 1970).

[3] Robert K. Merton, *Social Theory and Social Structure*, 1968 enlarged ed. (New York: Free Press, 1968), pp. 1–68.

[4] W. S. Gilbert recognized this many years ago in the character of the "fleshly poet," Bunthorne, in *Patience*.

Parsons, attempted to provide an over-all framework in which sociology could develop. Although some fruitful research emerged from this perspective, the reaction of sociologists to such overarching approaches was largely antagonistic. While some sociologists wrote learned critical articles, nonsociologists simply snickered as they watched sociologists bury the world and themselves in abstruse terminologies which, like the tools and techniques, were far removed from honest-to-goodness interacting people. The "higher level of abstraction" that sociologists sought soared into the stratosphere.

So the sociologist-as-scientist looked for Truth and thought he found it in grand theory or stupendous method. As it turned out, however, and as the sociologist should have realized, "truth" was far more elusive; it bore the stamp of the country or group in which the sociologist practiced. There was American "truth" and Russian "truth" and military "truth" and that of whoever else was paying the freight. When any sociologist left the comparative safety of his book-lined cubicle to observe the reality in which he pursued his "truth" and admitted that what he saw was relative to a particular sociopolitical ideology, as did the late C. Wright Mills, he was viewed with suspicion by many. In their zeal to emulate Weber's ethical neutrality, sociologists neglected another crucial facet of Weber's thought—the decisive interconnection between ideology and action, even scientific action.

By and large, until very recently, the sociologist has failed to confront the values that guide his research. So intent has he been on legitimating his place within the firmament of the sciences that this concern has dominated his self-perception and, consequently, his perception of the world about him. Now, assuredly it is difficult to confront any set of values, particularly the values that guide one's work, for the analysis of presuppositions implies distrust of them. And he who distrusts the normative system in which he must operate obviously has difficulty operating effectively, unless, of course, he chooses to "play the game" regardless of personal convictions. In the former situation his peers may suspect him; in the latter case he will have to live with himself. In either case he suffers both personally and professionally.

Increasingly, then, sociologists have been urging upon their colleagues what has been called a "reflexive"—by which is meant "reflective"—sociology.[5] This is a plea for a sociology that is continually self-conscious and critical of itself as a discipline, that sees theory and research as hand-in-glove and ties both to an involvement with living human beings, coping with an intensely problematic world. It is a demand for a sociology that is "radical" in the best traditions of sociology's founding fathers. The sociologists who take this position suggest that it is not enough to take an ethically neutral cop-out. It is inadmissible that the sociologist should say, as he has said: I have knowledge; here it is to be used—by others. Advocates of a reflexive, radical sociology assert that the sociologist is obliged to cry out for a better human condition and to use his knowledge to make reality of man's dreams and hopes. He ought not to accept the values of society because they have the sanction of tradition about them. Rather, say these advocates, the sociologist as a man of knowledge can test social values in the crucible of research. He can question the correspondence of these values either to the reality of social existence or to the aspirations of citizens, of nations, and of human beings. In short, there is no contradiction between scholarly rigor and humanitarian impulses. In fact, both ends are served when the sociologist not only recognizes the climate of values that structure his work but makes them explicit. The sociologist would then be able to recapture the spirit of "the real Weber"—the man of action as well as intellectual detachment—which has been well-nigh lost in the drive for the respectability of the label "scientist."

[5] Gouldner, *Coming Crisis in Western Sociology*, pp. 481–512.

A by-product of such an orientation would be the freedom of the sociologist-scholar from the necessity to conform to a particular sociological party line. He would no longer have to follow particular research models or particular lines of inquiry because of fashion or expedient or, simply, the necessity of survival in brutal academia. It is claimed that the sociologist could then be really creative because he could follow his curiosity wherever it might lead without having to worry about consequences. His only guide to the worth of a problem would be its interest for him, as well, of course, as its contribution to enhancement of the human potential.

Notwithstanding these parochial concerns, there is no question that sociology appears to have forgotten about people. It is perhaps ironic that the more the sociologist learns, the farther removed he is from his data. In part this is a function of the use of statistical techniques. The larger the number of cases with which we can work, assuming that they were randomly selected in the first place, the higher the probability that these cases (the sample) adequately represent the population from which they were drawn. The responses of the sample should ideally mirror the responses of the total population; the larger the sample, the greater should be the correspondence (allowing for some unavoidable variation between samples) to the limiting case where the sample and the total population are identical. Now, given the resources of time and money, it becomes relatively easy to obtain individual responses to questionnaires or interviews or whatever. Computers make it easy to analyze these responses. It is more difficult to design the interview schedule or the observation protocol or attitude inventory that will get at what the investigator desires to learn, but even this can be accomplished in time. Yet throughout the whole data-generating and data-gathering process the investigator will probably never see the people behind the punches in the IBM cards or the bits of information on the magnetic tape. The small-scale study in which the researcher conducts his own in-depth interviews or participates in the life of the social organization in which he is interested is largely out of fashion because the results of such studies appear to lack the respectability of larger and seemingly more sophisticated enterprises; it is frequently difficult to find the funds to conduct such a one-man operation. Consequently, much sociological analysis is carried on in comparative isolation. The sociologist may "know about" the people whose behavior he purports to understand but have precious little "acquaintance with" them. His findings therefore often turn out to have little correspondence with the real world of his subjects and hence have a sterile, even lifeless, quality about them.

I suppose that this state of affairs results from the historical dilemma in which the field currently finds itself. On the one hand, there is the tradition of Comte and Durkheim. A "positive," scientific understanding of society will come only when one keeps the rigor of the scientific method and the precision of mathematics firmly in mind. But, on the other hand, there is a tradition that opts for a reformist and reportorial slant: Tell a story with all possible attention to the human element, attempt to make a difference in people's lives, and build a body of knowledge in the process. It must then be asked whether these two traditions in fact represent incompatible alternatives to the achievement of a bona fide science of sociology or, rather, are simply two sides of the same coin. As I see the field I must argue for the latter case.

A "fact" is nothing more than a meaningful relation between phenomena suggested by and verified through the use of a particular theoretical position. One cannot divorce the empirical data that generate "facts" from the social and cultural environments in which the data are found without divesting them of whatever interpretive or predictive value they might have. Although it may be true that one need not *be* Caesar in order to understand him (as Weber put it), nevertheless empathy, concern, involvement—precisely what

Weber called "understanding"—in the sociocultural matrices of one's subjects is a fundamental prerequisite to that understanding which, in the scientific sense, leads to "facts," their interrelationship, and ultimately to meaningful generalization and the accumulation of a body of knowledge. Unless a sociologist is completely insensitive, he must at some point realize that if he is to comprehend what he studies he must consider the why's as well as the ways of behavior. He must be aware of the values, concerns, and problems that provide a backdrop for behavior. Consequently, he will recognize that research "pays off" only when it proceeds from and, so to speak, feeds back into those very problems and concerns.

I want to state the case as clearly as possible. The sociological craft—indeed, the central challenge of the field—is a commitment not merely to conceptual mastery or even methodological wizardry but to solution of the problems that appear to bedevil people trying to live in and make sense of their environment of things and other humans. I am convinced that only in this way can the sociologist gather knowledge that will be "relevant" for a fragmented and fearful world and that, in the final analysis, will make the sociologist useful to that world and eventually to himself. It is sometimes said that the sociologist cannot serve the twin masters of scholarly rigor and that imprecision which is the essence of our humanity. Perhaps he serves each better when he serves them both, profiting thereby both as sociologist and as citizen.

But the debate goes on. Opposed to those who urge a sociology more reflective on itself and more responsive to human needs are those who label such a plea as much too partisan for value-free science, who assert that it smacks of an unhealthy radicalism. Yet, like the blind men who each characterized an elephant in terms of the particular portion of anatomy they "examined," the advocates of the opposing views are partly in the right as well as partly in the wrong.

Certainly, to regard those who speak for a reassessment of research priorities and an awakening ideological sensitivity as dissidents, despoilers, and malcontents is narrow-minded at the very least. Students of change can hardly be unmindful of calls for change from within their ranks. Sociology does indeed represent a radical departure in the analysis of social conduct in that it assumes such conduct to be susceptible of understanding and direction—precisely because the behavior is emergent and creative. The sociological orientation that man makes his environment rather than responds to it in some kind of deterministic fashion is still a novel conception even at this late date. So sociology is radical and the sociologist must be society's gadfly, because the questioning of behavior even as one watches it take shape implies suspicion of the behavior. Were sociology to do less, it would debase its heritage. However, it is equally clear that the frustrated and disaffected sociologists who, in calling for the emergence of the field from a conservative straitjacket, argue that they cry alone in a defoliated intellectual wilderness, who claim they preach a new sociological dispensation, have lost or have yet to develop an appreciation of the history of their discipline. Their plaint is not new. It was voiced at the turn of the century, in the 'twenties, and following World War II. One could, if one wanted, see this concern in the writings of Comte. Thus, each side hurls its sticks and stones at the other, and current gatherings of sociologists hear updated versions of charge and countercharge. Where all this will end is an open question, but this is the state of affairs. If it strikes you as overblown or perhaps just naïve, remember that what is at stake in this debate is the basic course this still young science is to chart for itself. In the past, men have been excommunicated for less.

Outside the walls of the sociologist's shop the controversy goes largely unnoticed. For those who absorb their world through the filter of communications media (which, I guess, includes most of us at least some of the time) or through scanning the shelves of their friendly neighborhood bookstore, this would appear to be the age of sociology. The sociologist's vocabulary has intruded into popular speech—think, for example, of *charisma, status, the Protestant Ethic*—sociologists and their findings are quoted or cited in a variety of contexts, relevant or not, and sociology is somehow regarded as a panacea: it has all the answers necessary to solve all the world's problems. Sociology classes are filled to overflowing. And we all wait expectantly for that eruption of genius. Certainly, sociologists have learned a great deal about the dynamics of social life. But I am afraid accounts of our successes are both premature and exaggerated.

Unless sociologists can decide who they are, what their mission may be, and how they propose to get there, the field may perish in a mire of verbiage. Sociological expertise ought not to be for sale to the highest bidder. Neither should the sociologist proclaim how individuals can or should act; all he can suggest is how, in the light of available information, the particular values espoused by some aggregation of people might be pursued. But to expect sociology to somehow usher in an age of sweet reason is arrogance in the extreme. If we don't know who we are, how can we be much good to anybody else?

Nevertheless, perhaps the most worthwhile use of sociological knowledge, possibly even the very future of the field, may not derive at all from the practicing professional sociologist. The person who has majored in sociology in college, or who may have taken only a few courses, will have at least absorbed a perspective on man that should enable him to do whatever he does in a more informed, disciplined fashion. He might see the world in a different light. He might even find himself.

And isn't that what education is all about?

For Further Reading:
A Selective View

BERGER, PETER L. *Invitation to Sociology: A Humanistic Perspective.* Garden City, N.Y.: Doubleday Anchor Books, 1963.
A brief, penetrating, and often witty approach to sociology as a technique for critical analysis of the world and one's place within it.

BIERSTEDT, ROBERT. "Sociology and Humane Learning," *American Sociological Review* 25 (February, 1960):3–9.
In his presidential address to the Eastern Sociological Society, Bierstedt maintained that the preoccupation with scientific method obscures another facet of sociological scholarship that ought to be used more than it has been: the illumination of social life by pushing some thesis to its extreme, to see whether a more cogent or relevant picture will emerge than through ethically neutral, objective research. And the "bigger the picture" the more significant will sociological findings be. Sociology is thus as much an art, within the humanistic disciplines, as it is a science.

CUZZORT, R. P. *Humanity and Modern Sociological Thought.* New York: Holt, Rinehart & Winston, 1969.
A literate attempt to present some basic and enduring concerns of sociology through a discussion of the writings of fourteen major figures in sociology and cultural anthropology, together with a closing chapter on the uses of sociological thought and a glossary.

HAMMOND, PHILLIP E., ed. *Sociologists at Work.* New York: Basic Books, 1964.
In these "essays on the craft of sociology" fourteen sociologists provide candid and illuminating descriptions of how they conduct research. One gets a clear picture of what it means, and takes, to be a sociologist.

NISBET, ROBERT A. *The Sociological Tradition.* New York: Basic Books, 1966.
A complex, technical, but eminently rewarding examination of what the author regards as five notions central to the sociological tradition: community, authority, status, the sacred, and alienation.

Index

147